Myanmar's Spring Revolution

Myanmar's Spring Revolution

Students, higher education and political change

Marie Lall and Ikuko Okamoto

UCLPRESS

First published in 2026 by
UCL Press
University College London
Gower Street
London WC1E 6BT

Available to download free: www.uclpress.co.uk

A CIP catalogue record for this book is available from the British Library.

ISBN: 978-1-80655-063-0 (Hbk)
ISBN: 978-1-80655-064-7 (Pbk)
ISBN: 978-1-80655-065-4 (PDF)
ISBN: 978-1-80655-066-1 (epub)
DOI: https://doi.org/10.14324/111.9781806550654

Dedicated to our academic families

Contents

List of figures and tables

Figures

Tables

List of abbreviations

AA	Arakan Army
ABSDF	All Burma Students' Democratic Front
ASEAN	Association of South East Asian Nations
BERA	British Educational Research Association
C3C	Central Command and Coordination Committee (NUG)
CBO	Community-based organisation(s)
CDC	Children's Development Centre
CDF	Chinland Defence Force
CDM	Civil Disobedience Movement
CM	Chiang Mai
CNF	Chin National Front
CR	Chiang Rai
CS	Chin State
EAO	Ethnic armed organisation(s)
EDC	Education Degree College(s)
EMPM	European Mobility Programme for Myanmar
ERO	Ethnic Revolutionary Organisation
FGD	Focus group discussion
GED	General Educational Development (test)
HEI	Higher education institution
IB	India border
ICG	International Crisis Group
ICT	Information and communication technology
IDP	Internally displaced person
INT	Interview
J2C	Joint Command and Coordination (NUG)
KAS	Konrad Adenauer Foundation
KEC	Kachin Education Consortium
KECD	Karen Education and Culture Department
KIA	Kachin Independence Army
KNDF	Karenni National Defence Force
KNPP	Karenni National Progressive Party
KNU	Karen National Union
KPDF	Kachin People's Defence Force
LDF	Local Defence Force(s)

LWS	London Writers' Salon
MDCs	Military Division Commands
MDEP	Myanmar Digital Education Platform
MECC	Migrant Education Coordination Centre
MJY	Mai Ja Yang
MLC	Migrant learning centre
MMK	Myanmar Kyat
MNDAA	Myanmar National Democratic Alliance Army
MS	Mae Sot
NAQAC	National Accreditation and Quality Assurance Committee
NGO	Non-governmental organisation
NMSP	New Mon State Party
NRC	(Myanmar) National Registration Card
NUG	National Unity Government
ODA	Overseas development aid
PDF	People's Defence Force(s)
RCDC	Regional Centre for Social Science and Sustainable Development (Chiang Mai University)
RCSS	Restoration Council of Shan State (Shan State Army South)
SAC	State Administration Council
SGPA	School of Governance and Public Administration
SPDC	State Law and Restoration Council
SSPP	Shan State Progressive Party (Shan State Army North)
SU	Spring University
TNLA	Ta'ang National Liberation Army
USIP	United States Institute of Peace
UWSA	United Wa State Army

Acknowledgements

The journey of this book started with the coup on 1 February 2021, in the middle of the COVID pandemic. After the initial shock had worn off, colleagues across higher education started to ask – what will happen to Myanmar's students? Over the past four years there have been many different forms of support for Myanmar students inside and outside the country. One of the most important schemes has been the EU-funded EMPM top-up scholarships that allowed students who had not been able to complete their degrees to do so in another ASEAN country. I was grateful to be part of the initial research team to help set this up, and the situational analysis I conducted on the Thai–Myanmar border was the start of what became a much larger project to collect the stories of those who had to flee their country. I was joined in the field by my colleague and friend Prof. Ikuko Okamoto and together over a number of trips we met many young people and organisations and collected their stories. I therefore want to thank Sebastian Gries, Stefan Hasse-Bergen and the whole EMPM team for involving me in EMPM, which allowed this project to start. I acknowledge the DAAD funding that made this initial research trip possible. The Center for Sustainable Development Studies at Toyo University made follow-on trips possible; I am grateful for having been granted a research affiliation with them for the last few years that I have been based in both Tokyo and London.

This is my third book on Myanmar – but because of the coup it is also a very different book – a book written from the outside, rather than from inside the country. It was made possible with the support of many new people I met on this journey, in particular by the brave students on the Thai–Myanmar border. As such, it is fitting to first thank all those who cannot be named for security reasons but who sat with me and Ikuko sharing their stories. I hope we do you justice in the way we are bringing your voices to the wider world.

Thanks also go to the student-led higher education institutions (HEIs) – Burma Academy, Irrawaddy Law School and Spring University Myanmar – whose founders and leaders met with us many times and allowed us to speak to their students. I am also grateful to Ma Ei Thin Zar, who has set up projects for fleeing students, houses them, feeds them and who facilitated several meetings with them. Without brave women like her, many of those on the run would have no one to turn to.

We are grateful to many education organisations who opened their doors to us, including Hsa Htoo Lei, Minmahaw, New Blood School, the Children's Development Centre (CDC) and Mae Taw Clinic where Dr Cynthia Maung took time to meet us, Teacher Focus and Regional Centre for Social Science and Sustainable Development (RCDC) at Chiang Mai University where we were able to meet with Prof. Chayan, whose work to protect Myanmar students and academics has been invaluable.

This book would not have been possible without the support of Ko Min Aung Mann, who was part of the research team, contacted our respondents, set up meetings and gathered data with us and for us. As a promising young academic, he was able to publish a separate article as part of the project.

Most academics will know what it feels like to have collected data, but to not know where or even how to get started with the writing. A year ago, after the death of a close friend, I realised that I seemed unable to write as before. Daniela Bak pulled me out of my hole by introducing me to the London Writers' Salon (LWS). It was through the daily practice of writing with 200+ other people that this book started taking shape. I am indebted both to her and LWS; without their help I am not sure this book would ever have been completed.

I am also grateful to Pat Gordon-Smith at UCL Press who has been my patient publisher for the last three books. I used to switch publishers for each book I wrote till I found a 'publishing home' within my own university. The open access model adopted by UCL Press means that the voices of our respondents will be available for free to anyone who is interested in Myanmar.

This book is dedicated to our academic families. Over the three decades of being an academic I have realised that the relationships forged with some colleagues go well beyond friendship and will last a lifetime. Across India, Pakistan, Myanmar, the UK and Japan my thanks go to AAT, Ali K., Alex L., Brad B., Camille K. H., Dave G., Geetha N., Jiva S., Keizo K., KPH, Licia P., Masayuki T., Saumen C. and Tania S., who have been a part of my academic journey and supported me every step of the way.

Final thanks – as always – to Viren, who has patiently put up with my many absences and for supporting my choice to live both in Japan and in the UK.

Marie Lall

I have long been engaged in research on the livelihoods of rural communities in Myanmar, conducting fieldwork across various regions of the country. The COVID-19 pandemic in 2020, followed by the coup in 2021, drastically altered the lives of these communities. At the same time, these events created a profound sense of uncertainty for me as a researcher, as it became increasingly difficult for me to visit the people whose lives I had closely followed for many years.

Since the mid-2010s, I have also been involved in higher education, teaching at university level and mentoring students. In the context of my growing engagement with education, I was fortunate to work on this project with my colleague and friend, Prof. Marie Lall. Through our collaborative fieldwork, we were able to listen to the voices of young people who had been forced to flee their country – young people who should have been at the centre of Myanmar's future. I am deeply grateful to have had the chance to help convey their stories to a wider audience through this book.

I would like to join Marie in expressing my sincere appreciation to all those who contributed to our research, especially the students and educators who shared their experiences with great courage. I am also grateful to Ko Min Aung Mann, who worked with us on this project and supported the research in many ways.

I also thank Dr Kota Watanabe, who facilitated my revisit to Mae Sot in 2022 after nearly 10 years and helped me reconnect with the situation in the border area before this collaborative research. I am equally grateful to Dr Suebsakun Kidnukorn at Mae Fah Luang University for his generous support in facilitating interviews with his students in early 2025.

I gratefully acknowledge the Center for Sustainable Development Studies at Toyo University for supporting this research through the Top Priority Research Program (2022–4) and Toyo University Top Priority Research Program Grant Number 2025T4. Part of my fieldwork was also supported by the Japan Society for the Promotion of Science (JSPS) KAKENHI (grant numbers 20K12376 and 23K28313).

Finally, I would like to express my heartfelt gratitude to my family. My husband, Jiro, has always supported me in taking on research trips, and I am also thankful to my son, Yuki, for his warm understanding. Their continued encouragement has meant a great deal throughout this journey.

Ikuko Okamoto

Figure 0.1 Map of Myanmar. Source: CartoGIS Services, College of Asia and the Pacific, The Australian National University.

Introduction

On 1 February 2021, Myanmar's military conducted a coup, putting to an end a decade of reforms (many of which were documented in the lead author's previous two books on the country). Although the third in Myanmar's history, the coup was received as a moral shock by a large part of Myanmar's population, and the response was an unprecedented resistance movement branded as the Spring Revolution by the activists leading it. Many – but not all – of the key resistance leaders were students and academics. As will be described later, this movement is characterised by Gen Z, the young people who were most affected by the coup. While what the world can see is a youth-led movement, this book is about the students and academics who played a leading role in the post-coup protests and who are still fighting the Myanmar military, both by taking up arms and by creating their own HEIs. Using Myanmar student voices from the border and inside Myanmar, the book explains why this time the resistance is different and why these students see this as a revolution that goes well beyond protesting against a military regime.

The book has three aims. The first is to give Myanmar students a place to voice their views on their Revolution and the future they are fighting for. In light of wars in Ukraine, Gaza and Iran, the conflict in Myanmar has largely been forgotten. The youth-led resistance that is fighting the Myanmar military seems to have no witnesses. This book is a way of giving voice to those most affected by the coup and those who are giving their lives for the future of their country. Given Myanmar's geographical location between India, China and the Association of Southeast Asian Nations (ASEAN), it is important to get a better understanding of the conflict and the fault lines that underpin it. The second aim, therefore, is to document and explain the underlying dynamics of one of the most complex state–society conflicts of the twenty-first century, to help a better understanding that for Myanmar there are no easy solutions – what might have been tried elsewhere is unlikely to work here. Myanmar is unique both in the makeup of its conflict, which encompasses domestic and international forces, and in the resistance this conflict has bred over decades of repression.

Myanmar came to prominence because it emerged from almost total isolation in the mid-2000s. There was a global push to support and a global rush to influence unprecedented reforms, which on the surface looked like a great success. The third aim is to give some insight into both why the reforms failed, and how these reforms were nevertheless important in creating the current resistance and Revolution. The book argues that it is because of the decade of reforms between 2010 and 2020 that this Revolution emerged and has sustained itself. The Revolution has led to an unprecedented understanding of unity and common cause across religious and ethnic faultlines among Myanmar's youth, resulting in the imaginary of a different country once the conflict ends.

Theoretical framework

The book offers three intertwined theoretical discussions that are important to understand political change in the twenty-first century, not only in Myanmar but also elsewhere, as seen in Figure 0.2 and explained in this section.

First, the book engages with a novel and unprecedented resistance movement that emerged out of Myanmar's universities. This resistance goes beyond an armed movement; rather, students have used education to fight back. As this book will show, some have developed online universities that offer higher education continuation to their peers both inside and outside the country. Students have historically been part of anti-establishment protests and this reflects an intersection of Foucault and Habermas' work on student resistance – Foucault focusing on how students challenge overt power structures and Habermas on how students create spaces for inclusive and non-coercive dialogues. Foucault's argument that power is not held by individuals or groups but is exercised through networks is a particularly good starting point. Resistance to the coup emerged from the universities and developed the Civil Disobedience Movement (CDM) network, where student relationships were the key driver. Using social media to underpin their

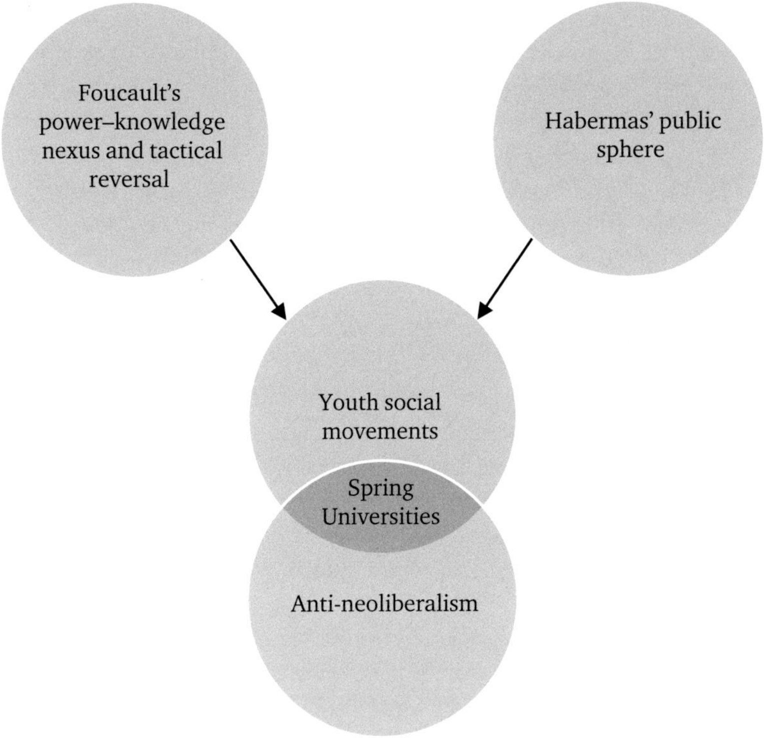

Figure 0.2 Theoretical framework. Source: Authors.

wide-ranging connections, students challenged the military power structure first through protests and then through the nationwide boycott of State Administration Council (SAC) institutions. This was followed by the taking up of arms and the creation of People's Defence Forces (PDFs) as well as asserting control of governance by the National Unity Government (NUG). However, there was also the appropriation of higher education by the students – a key difference from previous protest movements. The focus of this book remains on the students and their heading up of higher education through digital tools,[1] exemplifying Foucault's tactical reversal. This book shows how in this tactical reversal, students asserted their agency to dominate the power–knowledge nexus and the narrative of the Revolution. The online universities discussed in Chapter 4 exemplify how alternative knowledge challenges the SAC's legitimacy in controlling Myanmar's education space. These students have understood that they need to change the Gramscian common sense that has underpinned Myanmar's military governance structure for decades and replace it with a narrative focused on democracy and inclusiveness. By doing so, Myanmar's students have not only resisted the Myanmar military regime with their bodies but also with their minds, through the creation of inclusive online higher education spaces to withstand the SAC. The Spring Universities therefore reflect Habermas' concept of a public sphere – a space where Myanmar students can freely discuss alternative futures for their country. In SAC-controlled universities such discussions are impossible. But the creation of the student resistance movement has led to a large number of debates, many of which are discussed in the following chapters.[2] The intersection of Foucault and Habermas' work form a sphere through which Myanmar's student resistance can be partially understood. Since this lens is grounded in a Western and historical tradition, it is insufficient to comprehend what has happened and (at the time of writing) continues to happen on the ground. In the era of social media, the texture of resistance has changed. There is a reason why this Revolution is depicted as novel and unprecedented – this Revolution has the 'knowledge making of resistance' at its heart, a process that is dynamic and perpetually changing, adapting and developing.[3]

Therefore, the second lens through which to analyse Myanmar's Spring Revolution is the role of youth movements in shaping politics in the Global South. As detailed by Novelli et al.'s book *Laboratories of Learning: Social Movements, Education and Knowledge-Making in the Global South* (2024), youth-led social movements are playing a central role in contemporary political change across Southeast Asia, yet their impact has not been fully recognised within academic scholarship. The protest movements in Thailand and Hong Kong served as a model for Myanmar's youth movement.[4] Novelli et al.'s book depicts how these new types of youth-led social movements can serve as spaces of learning and knowledge making in which activists develop new resistance strategies through practice and reflection, spreading them to other movements through social media. They include all young people, not only students. But those who might not be students learn from the network and contribute to the knowledge making. Novelli et al.'s framework shows how transformative pedagogies not only focus on learning but also on challenging social power structures, creating new forms of organisation, allowing for diverse voices and points of view to be heard and cultivating an inclusive sphere. Myanmar's student movement, and in particular the Spring Universities, are an example of how transformative pedagogies both allow for a more inclusive debate and resist traditional power structures; not only of the SAC, but also in certain cases the traditional views propagated by certain members of the NUG. As shall be seen in subsequent chapters, the student movement has allowed for ethnic minority views to be heard and accepted; the role of women, often marginalised in Myanmar's social movements, has been prominent, and for the first time young people have recognised the rights of Rohingyas. The internet and social media space are a key part of this, shaping the movements differently from those that served as models for Habermas and Foucault. One can think of this as the upgraded Foucault–Habermas lens, or the Foucault–Habermas framework on steroids. The book therefore uses this updated view as a lens through which to interpret Myanmar's Spring Revolution. While this sphere can help readers engage with the wider anti-regime resistance as depicted in Chapters 2 and 3, it is not in itself sufficient to explain what has happened in Myanmar's revolutionary higher education space. A third lens is required, one generally ignored by the literature engaging with the Spring Revolution – the role and meaning of higher education in a neoliberal world and its role in resisting not only the dictatorship but also the neoliberal logic of global higher education.

At a time when neoliberal tendencies in education are at their peak, the revolutionary students offer courses so that their peers both inside and outside of Myanmar are able to continue their education. In so doing, they question the marketplace of higher education. As shall be seen in Chapter 4, they see higher education as a space for political change driven from the bottom up, very much contesting the contemporary neoliberal logic that intersects human capital theory with higher education profit-making motives. While realising the need for skills and students needing to get jobs to be able to survive, the courses on offer by the three Spring Universities reflect a desire to use higher education for inclusive nation building and critical thinking to challenge the traditional structures of both politics and education. All of the student-led HEIs offer courses on social justice and democracy; there is an emphasis on the social sciences. Both are seen as key pillars for rebuilding a better, more just Myanmar. Their governance models are flat rather than hierarchical. While they look to international universities for recognition and accreditation of their work, they resist Western structures, including trying to avoid student fees in their belief that higher education is for all and is a necessity for the rebuilding of Myanmar. This anti-neoliberal stand is not only focused on what they offer and what they believe Myanmar universities should look like when the Spring Revolution succeeds, but also vested in a critique of the universities in the countries they have fled to – in particular Thailand. As shall be seen in Chapter 5, many students question why universities in Thailand did not offer them sanctuary and the opportunity to complete their studies. The question of what responsibilities universities have when faced with displaced and fleeing students is at the heart of the creation of the Spring Universities and central to their contestation of the neoliberal higher education model. By channelling their protest in this way, these students go beyond Myanmar's Spring Revolution and offer an alternative vision of resistance to the wider world.

Whilst the book remains grounded in fieldwork, the framework that has just been described offers insights into this knowledge-making resistance movement, which forms part of a wider range of youth-led social movements that intersect with higher education, political change and neoliberal logic. This helps make meaning of what is happening on the ground. The conclusions of each chapter return to the framework, focusing on how the students' narrative and actions contribute to the 'knowledge making of resistance' both in terms of resistance to the dictatorship and resistance to the accepted neoliberal logic of higher education. In a landscape where there is perpetual change and movement, applying these lenses will help disentangle the complex web of data and the core of the three intersecting lenses will help explain the drivers for the Spring Revolution.

Data and fieldwork

The book is based on in-person fieldwork on the Thai–Myanmar border and remote data collection with students inside Myanmar through a survey and online interviews with around 200 current/former students as well as another 50 respondents including current/former academics, and respondents working in education-related organisations. The initial fieldwork in Thailand was conducted on two trips in February and November 2023. Follow-on data was collected online in Thailand and in person on the India–Myanmar border (in the border towns between Mizoram, India and Chin State, Myanmar) in 2024, and in person again in Thailand in early 2025. One of the authors also travelled briefly to Myanmar in 2025, informally recording impressions that have been integrated into the narrative.

The three data chapters and the Epilogue draw on different parts of the data collected. Chapter 3 is based on focus group discussions (FGDs) with students and interviews with migrant support organisations and other civil society organisations that have been supporting education on the Thai–Myanmar border, as well as a survey of students inside

Myanmar, most of which was collected on the first trip. It also incorporates Licia Proserpio's writing on the India–Myanmar border to describe the students who left their homes to build the resistance movement. Chapter 4 is based on in-person meetings and interviews with the founders of all three student-led HEIs, as well as discussions with students benefitting from their courses. The founders were interviewed on both initial trips and re-interviewed with the help of a local researcher a third time to understand the progress of their HEIs. In addition, this chapter draws on interviews with alternative education organisations developed by former academics and the NUG. Chapter 5 and the Epilogue are based on in-person FGDs collected on the second trip and online and in-person interviews with students on the Thai and India borders and inside Myanmar in the course of 2024 and 2025. Interviews were conducted in Burmese and English, at times with the help of a local researcher. In order to maintain the anonymity and safety of our respondents, the labelling of the respondents' quotes only indicates their location (MS for Mae Sot, CM for Chiang Mai, CR for Chiang Rai, IB for India Border) and whether these were collected as a part of an FGD, an interview (INT) or as part of the survey. For the quotes emanating from the student-led HEIs, SU (Spring University) is used as an acronym. Ethics approval was received from the UCL Institute of Education, based on the British Educational Research Association (BERA) guidelines. Respondents were informed that all data would be anonymised and about their right to withdraw at any time before the end of each data collection trip conducted.

The data covers a wide range of views on the Spring Revolution as well as the role and purpose of higher education both as part of the resistance and as a foundation for building a new country. The respondents were clear that they wanted their views to be made public so that the world might not forget Myanmar and might support them in the quest for a more just and democratic future.

Content

This book is divided into five main chapters, followed by an Epilogue.

Chapter 1 sets the scene by summarising what led to a decade of reforms and describing the reforms themselves. It also engages with the importance of higher education in Myanmar politics, the government and international politics that underpinned higher education, its reform between 2012 and 2020 and the anti-regime protests that emerged from it. It is based on the previous UCL Press publication by Lall (2021a) about the education reforms in Myanmar, which relied on almost two decades of data collected by the lead author from dozens of field trips across the country between 2005 and 2019.

Chapter 2 details the coup and the public reaction to it. The coup took place in the early hours of 1 February 2021, just before the newly elected Members of Parliament of the 2020 elections were about to take their seats in parliament. The coup led to widespread protests, headed initially by students and staff in the higher education sector and subsequently joined by others, such as teachers, union members, garment workers and so on. The state response was a nationwide crackdown that has taken Myanmar onto a path of civil war. This was not the first time that the *Tatmadaw* – as the Myanmar military is known – had reacted violently to protests. Similar repressions happened in 1962, 1988, 1990 and 2007. The chapter locates the most recent coup, and how the resistance started on Myanmar's higher education campuses, in the wider history of higher education-led resistance in the country, giving some background on how students led previous anti-regime protest movements. It details how students and the wider higher education sector have always faced suffering, with years of closures and academic repression. It also explains how in the eyes of the military, higher education is not a necessary element of wider reforms but rather an education system that should teach young people to respect the military and its position. Those who disrespect them, the military maintains, are in revolt against the stalwarts of the nation. This chapter is largely based on secondary sources and news articles, as well as many informal conversations with and emails from Myanmar colleagues and friends who lived through the coup and its aftermath.

Chapter 3 details different forms of resistance, modes of survival and the challenges faced by students in Myanmar and in exile. It explains how the protesting students cannot be seen as homogeneous and that their differing situations inform how they take part in the resistance. The research uncovered big differences between students from middle-class families and those from more modest backgrounds, including students whose parents were from poor rural areas. The chapter also discusses how the coup engaged students who had not been active in the student unions versus those who had been active in previous protests during the reforms period. The coup brought together many different students who share the hardships by living and supporting each other regardless of their social, ethnic and religious backgrounds. The chapter therefore engages with the identity of the respondents, how they see themselves, their mission and the future of their country, all tied to their student identity. While this chapter does engage with some of the armed resistance and the role of the PDFs, it focuses more on those who have left Myanmar – in particular students – and are working for the Revolution on Myanmar's borders using education as a tool to change the country.

Chapter 4 delves into the world of higher education after the coup and describes how students have created online education opportunities for other students both inside and outside Myanmar. This is the first instance of refugee students creating HEI platforms for internally displaced as well as other refugee students. It maps the activities of the Spring Universities three years after the coup, focusing on specific case studies: the Burma Academy, the Spring University Myanmar and Irrawaddy Law School. In doing so, this chapter shows the educational re-imagining that these institutions are creating. These institutions, one of which has over 40,000 registered students, have a set of cornerstones that shape how curricula are structured: the imperative to focus teaching content around discourses on inclusion, intersectionality and social justice; the importance of debating contemporary issues around Myanmar federalism, community building and peacekeeping in educational spaces; the importance of fostering a research culture based on action-research practices and community-based research; and a better teaching and learning experience supported by the savvy use of IT tools and social media. It delves into the aims of the founders, how they see their work in terms of the future of their country and Myanmar's future higher education. The chapter also engages briefly with other alternative higher education provision that has emerged after the coup. This includes what the NUG's ministry of education has been able to offer as well as the actual (and planned) expansion of ethnic higher education that aims to offer opportunities to the ethnic nationality youth, in particular those graduating from ethnic armed group-operated schools.

Chapter 5 gives voice to the students who are leading the Spring Revolution. The changed higher education system the students want for themselves and for Myanmar has to do with learning and acquiring knowledge, but also with resilience and resistance – it is the fundamental basis for the Revolution. This chapter engages with the voices of the students waging war against the Myanmar regime recounting how they conceive the Revolution and the role of higher education in the Revolution. It also discusses their views on the future of Myanmar and the kind of country they want to build. It argues that this Revolution would have been impossible without the preceding decade of reforms that formed the views of students and instilled in them a sense of 'rights'. The concept of 'rights' as it is understood in Western society is relatively recent in Myanmar. The reforms were accompanied by freedom of expression and freedom of movement, shifting young people's views as to what they could expect from the state. Students who entered university a decade after the reforms began to have a sense of rights, and *this* is what makes them different from earlier generations. The coup took those rights away. Students expressed a variety of ways in which they felt their individual rights were violated, and then how they transitioned to seeing that they had a larger responsibility towards their country. Some were prompted by the fact that they were losing their education and, with this, they had been robbed of their future.

The book ends with an Epilogue that gives the latest update on the Spring Revolution before publication and reflects on the student journeys in the 3–4 years that have passed since the country was irrevocably changed by the military-led third coup. It also engages with the rift between those who supported the Revolution and those who did not, and the prospects of continued resistance as seen by the students themselves. Lastly it updates the volume in light of the massive earthquake that struck near Mandalay in March 2025 and the SAC's plan for elections.

Notes

1 As opposed to all the other resistance groups that have been a part of the Spring Revolution.
2 It is interesting to note that the student-led space allows for a much freer discussion of the future of the country than the spheres created by the NUG, which believes that the NLD's win during the 2020 elections gave them the right to lead the resistance and determine the narrative – in that way partially emulating the military dictatorship. However, in the student-led spaces, debates thrive and a wide palette of views are expressed.
3 We use Novelli et al.'s 'Knowledge Making in Social Movements' and have adapted this here as the 'knowledge making of resistance' – a core part of the Myanmar youth-led social resistance and Spring Revolution.
4 When adding Myanmar it is dubbed the 'Milk Tea Alliance'.

1

A decade of reforms

This chapter summarises the events that led to a decade of reforms and the role of higher education in Myanmar politics. It is based on almost two decades' worth of data collected by the lead author across dozens of field trips across the country between 2005 and 2019. While this book shares its background with an earlier UCL Press publication by Lall (2021a) on the education reforms in Myanmar, this chapter focuses more specifically on some of the political aspects that have underpinned higher education, its reform and the anti-regime protests that emerged from it.

Myanmar's first two military coups, education and student protests

In the 78 years since Myanmar achieved independence from Britain in 1948, it has faced three military takeovers: in 1962, 1988 and 2021. All of them have been countered by student protests. Metro (2016) argues that such demonstrations are linked to the country's history, as students have protested for decades not only on education issues, but also on social and economic issues. The Myanmar coup d'état on 2 March 1962 marked the beginning of Tatmadaw political dominance in Myanmar. In 1962, the Tatmadaw replaced the civilian and democratic government led by Prime Minister U Nu with the Union Revolutionary Council. The leader of the coup, General Ne Win, resigned from his military rank on 20 April 1972 and became U Ne Win, the civilian premier of the country, together with 20 of his top supporters (Butwell 1972). Myanmar, then known as Burma, would be ruled for 26 years by General Ne Win and his Burma Socialist Program Party (BSPP), in which he acted as chair and established one-party rule. In 1962, university students were among the most active to protest against the General Ne Win-led military coup. On 9 May 1962, the Rangoon University Act was invalidated by the Revolutionary Council after it took over the administration of the university. On 7 July, approximately 2,000 students from Rangoon University (now called Yangon University) protested in response. The protests in Rangoon University were against stricter campus regulations, the end of the system of university self-administration and the new military regime. The main protests took place on 7 and 8 July 1962. The Tatmadaw responded by bombing the Student Union building, leading to the deaths of several students. According to Nang Mo Lao Rives (2014), cited in Proserpio (2025), the demolition of buildings that were used for political meetings was a repression tactic of Ne Win's government. This shows the intention of destroying any political dissent at the root by taking away the space in which it could be discussed. However, these tactics only reinforced the fact that the fulcrum of Myanmar politics lay within universities and that the demand for political change would from then on always emerge from students. In order to control students in the Ne Win era, teachers had to become 'agents of the state' and their main role was to deliver the curricular content dictated by the Council of University Academic Bodies without questioning its content and to monitor and exercise political control over students (Proserpio 2025). Student politics and protests were made as difficult as possible. Nevertheless, according to Egreteau (2009), students who could not pay their fees did protest in the 1970s and 1980s.

The new military regime made changes to the university system to tighten their control of higher education. Mandalay University, which had been established as a separate university in 1958, and Yangon University were placed directly under state control in 1963. A year later, the technical faculties of Education, Engineering, Economics and Medicine were removed from both Yangon and Mandalay Universities and given degree-awarding powers as separate technical and professional institutions, leaving both universities with the liberal arts, science and law. In effect, the amalgamation of HEIs brought about in previous years was reversed, creating a larger number of smaller, specialist universities. In dividing the student body and faculty, this served the political purposes of the regime, but it must also be seen in its historical and regional context – in India, for example, schools of science, schools of engineering and medical schools were set apart from other universities. The 1973 University Education Law consolidated the new division between arts and science universities and technical institutes (CESR 2013, p. 4).

The same University Education Law explicitly deprived HEIs of financial autonomy. As with other state institutions, universities' budget estimates had to be approved by the state and all expenditures had to be consistent with state-approved norms (CESR 2013, p. 7). Ultimately, the easy way to control HEIs was through their budgets.

Ne Win's Socialism in One Country Programme also initiated a programme of 'Burmanisation' that went well beyond the politics of education, but relied on both basic and higher education as a vehicle for its propagation. Burmanisation – based on the belief that the country needed a unifying national identity based on one culture, one language and one religion – was the hallmark of post-1962 education. Since independence, there had been conflict with separatist ethnic movements on the Thai and Chinese borders. These conflicts provided the reasons both for the 1962 military coup ('to prevent the disintegration of the nation') and for the process of forcing Burmanisation on all non-Bamar ethnic groups across the country. While Bamar-centred nationalism did not suddenly appear with the coup, after 1962, schools had to serve as an aid for the realisation of the revolutionary government's socialist and nationalist goals. Schools were nationalised, Burmese was made the official language of instruction, Buddhism the national religion and minority languages were removed from state schools. The aim was to force a unitary Bamar-dominated national identity upon all ethnicities (Houtman 1999; Thant Myint-U 2001; Lall 2021a). The forced assimilation process of Burmanisation excluded the cultures and languages of over 100 ethnic groups that comprise modern Burma. This, of course, also affected universities. The language of instruction in higher education was English (British Academy and École Française d'Extrême-Orient 2015),[1] the matriculation examination taken to enter university was in Burmese. The imposition of Burmese as the only language of instruction in all schools resulted in a larger dropout of ethnic students, whose mother tongues were different. As a result, universities came to have a proportionally lower intake of ethnic nationality students compared to Bamar students, resulting in turn in large gaps between Bamar and other ethnic groups when it came to jobs and income. The legacy of Ne Win's Burmanisation was never properly reversed, even with the education reforms after 2015.

After two and a half decades under General Ne Win's governance, in 1988, the spark of nationwide protests was again ignited at one of Myanmar's universities – Yangon Technological University. The revolt ultimately resulted in the unseating of Ne Win and led to the 8888 nationwide pro-democracy movement, named for 8 August 1988, when crowds of around one million went onto the streets to demonstrate. According to Lintner (1990), the start of the protests lay in a teashop brawl over the preferential treatment of a student whose father was a BSPP representative. This triggered demonstrations that were met with police violence, leading to more protests and more arrests. One protest on a bridge a few days later was met by armed soldiers, resulting in an unknown number of deaths. The demonstrations continued and morphed into protests against the BSPP's 25 years of economic mismanagement. As the arrests and killings of students continued, popular support across the country swung behind the student moment asking for regime change.[2] Ordinary citizens of all walks of life, including civil servants and businesspeople, were galvanised by the economic and social problems that the BSPP had created (Kyaw Yin Hlaing 2007). Western media was used to spread the information internationally (Lintner 1990). The resignation of General Ne Win (first replaced by General Sein Lwin and later by Dr Maung Maung) did not calm the protests. The demonstrators no longer asked merely for a change of leadership but started to demand a multi-party democratic system. Retaliatory violence spread across Yangon with protesters attacking policemen and informers, six of whom were beheaded (Egreteau 2009). This culminated in the protests on 8.8.88, during which the army shot live ammunition into the crowds, killing scores.[3]

Three important things emerged from the killings that day. First, as described by a number of analysists, a cohesive community of people bound together by sacrifice (*anitnah*) for the nation (Thein-Lemelson 2021 in Proserpio 2025) emerged, coalescing around the NLD and what would come to be known as the 88 Generation. The solidarity within this generation is what kept the spirit of the anti-junta movement alive both within the country and outside of it. This leads to the second outcome: the movement, repressed inside the country, moved to the Thai border and beyond, creating a transnational pro-democracy movement with members and supporters across the West as well as in Canada, Australia, the US and the UK. This movement, which included the All Burma Students' Democratic Front or ABSDF, born in November 1988, did not necessarily include the ethnic nationality refugees, also on the Thai border, but was a more Bamar-centric movement created and maintained by the students (and later also their children) who had fled after the protests were brutally repressed (Matelski 2016). They used transnational advocacy strategies to galvanise foreign governments in supporting sanctions against the government, many of which lasted until the reforms began in 2012. As many, including Proserpio (2025), have pointed out, the student leaders of the 1988 uprising – the 88 Generation – have a special status in Myanmar to this day. There is, however, a third outcome of the protests that took place over 30 years ago: the sense across today's Gen Z that their parents had failed. The fact that despite the sacrifices, killings and torture the Tatmadaw prevailed meant that the 2021 coup was possible. As will be seen in the subsequent chapters, members of 'Gen Z' emphasise that this time things cannot end as they did in 1988; they will have to fight – and die – until the Tatmadaw is removed from power and politics.

The student protests in the late 1980s and 1990s resulted in the closures of universities for extended periods. The duration of these closures differed from place to place. In Yangon, universities were closed for 10 of the 12 years from 1988 to 2000. In light of the protests, the government decided to relocate much of the country's undergraduate education provision to outside of the urban centres, making it harder for students to engage in politics. A number of these institutions were new HEIs registered with other ministries. Mandalay and Yangon Universities lost their undergraduate programmes (CESR 2013, p. 5). Universities that had been isolated from the rest of the world throughout the 'Burmese Way to Socialism' years became even more isolated. Myanmar academics had very little opportunity to go abroad and foreigners were not allowed on any of the campuses. Only a few academics received scholarships to complete doctorates, mainly in Japan, returning to teach in the Myanmar system upon return. Without access to international research, new books, journals and the internet, Myanmar's HEIs devolved into rote learning via set textbooks without any research input or innovation. Laboratories were under-resourced, libraries stocked obsolete or out-of-date materials and teaching spaces were old and dusty. The universities deteriorated rapidly.

The country continued to experience isolation during the 1990s through to the early 2000s. After the brutal crackdown on student protests, punitive sanctions were imposed by the West. There was limited interaction with Myanmar's eastern neighbours, but economic ties did improve with both ASEAN countries and China when the junta decided on some limited market-oriented reforms in the 1990s. However, Myanmar received no international aid. Apart from UNICEF and the Japan International Cooperation Agency (JICA), international aid and development agencies had virtually no role to play in the country. The sanctions and the lack of aid meant that Myanmar's public services, in particular education, quickly declined (Tonkin 2007; Wilson 2016). Since private education was illegal, families had no choice but to send their children to very poor-quality government schools followed by government higher education, which closely resembled the school system in terms of its teaching methodology.

Education before the reforms

Given the tight control of the SPDC over all aspects of Myanmar's governance, the entire education system was government-run, with the Ministry of Education imposing its curriculum in a very hierarchical top-down manner. Baseline data collected before the start of the reforms of 2010–11 showed that, from around 1.1 million new entrants to Grade 1 each year, only around 300,000 reached Grade 11, two thirds of whom failed matriculation annually (Education Management and Information Systems study, cited in Lall 2021a). Since entrance to university depends on students' scores in the matriculation exam, taken in Grade 11 at the age of 16, only a small percentage of the population ever made it to higher education. In Myanmar, access to basic education did not necessarily allow for social mobility due to structural inequalities that are exacerbated by class and the urban/rural divide, so prominent in a society whose economy has been dominated by agriculture. UNESCO (Symaco and Hayden 2024) estimated that 48.1 per cent of the richest quintile access universities, whilst only 1.2 per cent of the poorest quintile have acquired tertiary education, even though it is free of charge and there is a large (albeit low-quality) distance higher education sector (more on unequal access to higher education follows). Whilst the UNESCO figures were collected during the reform period (earlier figures are not available), they demonstrate the deep educational inequalities in Myanmar, despite decades of so-called socialist policies. For the poor, education has been offered by Buddhist monasteries in monastic schools, generally only at primary level. Whilst students are able to transfer to state schools for secondary provision, most are too poor to do so, limiting their chances to access higher education. Buddhist principles have always played an important role across the system, and not only in monastic institutions: in fact, Buddhism served as social glue and as a means of keeping civil society alive under military rule (Lorch 2007). The traditional Buddhist principles for education – social harmony, conformity and passivity – are very much reflected across the Myanmar educational system. Teachers were (and still are) badly paid; they serve society according to the Buddhist principles of seva (selfless service) and dana (generosity/charity). Buddhism as a philosophy and the Buddhist values of service to society deeply permeates the whole educational system, from primary to university levels. Teachers at schools and universities are revered by their students and their families for their role in offering 'enlightenment' and knowledge. This is particularly visible at the annual Sayar Gadaw Pwe (Homage Paying Ceremony) held during the month of Thadingyut, where students reaffirm their respect for their teachers.

Myanmar's universities have operated quite differently from most other higher education systems across the world. Centralisation has been a dominant feature from the outset and universities have lacked autonomy. As in schools, curricula and student assessments have traditionally been set by the Ministry of Education. The two Departments of Higher Education manage, respectively, universities in Lower Myanmar and in Upper Myanmar and are responsible for the administration and coordination of HEIs. Although a number of universities sit under different ministries, the 1973 University Education Law provided that academic matters were managed by two councils, both chaired by the Minister of Education: the Universities' Central Council, in charge of broad policy framing; and the Council of University Academic Bodies, responsible for academic regulations and the coordination of academic work. The National Education committee, formed in 1991, oversaw the two councils, making sure that educational policies were implemented. This structure made sure that universities had no autonomy, and rectors were always appointed by the government. Universities are located both in the urban centres of Yangon and Mandalay and in the regional and state capitals, as well as other smaller cities and rural/remote areas. All university staff are public servants and are centrally appointed by the Ministry of Education. A transfer/rotation system means that they change posts every few years, moving from one university to another around the country. This made any anti-government movement at staff level difficult; it also made setting up research teams to ensure the continuity of inquiry in research impossible. Staff sent to unfamiliar, sometimes remote locations experienced high levels of job dissatisfaction, which likely affected teaching delivery as well (Zue Wadi Htun in Symaco and Hayden 2024). Nevertheless, there are large differences between regional universities in remote areas (especially in ethnic states) and urban institutions. For example, universities in ethnic states often have some local staff who are not necessarily rotated as part of the national system, which bars them from the apex universities of Yangon and Mandalay. This centralised 'command and control' system resulted in strict hierarchies, with many senior academics worried about taking decisions that might be counter to the Ministry's wishes.

The teaching at Myanmar universities has traditionally been textbook based, partly because of the 'command and control' system described previously, and partly due to the lack of research that staff have been able to conduct. As in schools, rote memorisation for exams has been a normal feature, with little space for questions and critical thinking. Most university faculty members have no training in pedagogical strategies or techniques (Lall 2021a). Their method of teaching often relies on translating passages from English textbooks, which they themselves may not fully understand. Tuition in English – a language that most students cannot speak or even understand, and that many of the academics do not master sufficiently either – meant that any HE reforms would have to address issues of curriculum, assessment and research to build staff capacity across the sector. The fact that Myanmar's HEIs had little access to information and communication technology (ICT) facilities, including email and library databases, caused the sector to lag behind that of all other Asian countries.

A programme for change: the role of civil society and higher education as a vehicle of empowerment

In the early 2000s, a seven-step road map was devised by General Khin Nyunt, who was a part of the State Law and Restoration Council (SPDC) leadership, to move the country from an absolute military dictatorship to a parliamentary system controlled by the Tatmadaw. This change was largely due to Myanmar's junta witnessing the widening gap between their country and the rest of ASEAN; the fact that they had been passed over when their turn came to take on ASEAN leadership also played a role. It was clear to all inside Myanmar that democracy would not be on offer (Lall 2016).[4] The Tatmadaw would keep tight control of all key political processes. Nevertheless, this period of change was a key inflection point for Myanmar. Education would prove to be an important vehicle for making the best possible use of the change process that was on offer.

As mentioned previously, in the early 2000s, there were hardly any academic links between Myanmar's universities and international HEIs or foreign academics, especially from the West. All contact between university staff and foreigners was tightly controlled. Myanmar academics needed approval from the Ministry of Education for any travel abroad and permission to invite any foreigners onto their campus. The only programme to support Myanmar academics was set up by

Dr Kyaw Yin Hlaing, a Myanmar academic who had completed his PhD at Cornell University in the US and who was at the time based at the National University of Singapore. It was limited to the social sciences – this, however, was seen as particularly important. Across Myanmar's universities, the social sciences had been even more tightly controlled than the sciences, largely because they might foster anti-regime thinking. There was, for example, no teaching of Political Science – only courses in International Relations were allowed. With financial support from the German political foundation Konrad Adenauer Stiftung (KAS), whose regional headquarters were in Kuala Lumpur, Malaysia, Dr Kyaw Yin Hlaing developed a programme to enable foreign (including Western) academics to come and teach intensive courses to Myanmar junior academics. After lobbying helpful regime contacts, Dr Kyaw Yin Hlaing and Professor Robert Taylor, a long-time Myanmar specialist, managed to get permission from the government for foreign academics to teach a summer programme at Myanmar universities. The programme ran for the first time in 2004, with international academics mainly based at National University of Singapore. The programme ran again two subsequent years and was instrumental in the creation of Myanmar Egress, a civil society organisation described subsequently (Lall 2016).

In the autumn of 2004 General Khin Nyunt was arrested and his intelligence bureau machinery replaced with new staff. This opened up unprecedented space for civil society in urban areas. Civil society groups were able to start operating in Yangon; this had been impossible before. Using the road map period as an opportunity,[5] one civil society organisation stood out – Myanmar Egress. It was created by a group of friends who had studied prior to the 1990 university closures and realised that the generation that followed theirs had not had access to much post-secondary education. If Myanmar was to change, people needed to be educated – in particular, middle-class urban people required access to some sort of post-secondary education that engaged with politics, economics and societal change. The hope was that the new parliamentary system would offer some form of wider participation, and that might provide a platform for those not directly connected to the military junta to contribute to policy making. In light of this they set up what became, de facto, Myanmar's first private HEI, with both long and short courses taught by domestic and international faculty (Lall 2016). The financial support of German political foundations was crucial. The theme that education would be essential for change in Myanmar reverberates across this book. As will be seen in subsequent chapters, this is also the leitmotiv for many contemporary revolutionaries, who are in effect walking in the footsteps of the Myanmar Egress founders – even if the use of technology today makes it look different.

In September 2007 Myanmar saw some unrest as monks started protesting first in Yangon, then across the country. As in 1988, the grievances were in the first instance economic, as the petrol subsidies had been abolished and bus fares had increased. Many Myanmar families in poor circumstances were unable to pay the bus fares. Food prices also increased as the fuel costs went up, giving rise to expressions of dissent.[6] The increasing poverty level had a serious enough effect on the alms the monks were receiving to draw them out onto the streets. What had started as sporadic protests evolved into larger political marches demanding the freeing of Daw Aung San Suu Kyi from house arrest. The West named this the 'Saffron Revolution', although these protests were quite different from what most would consider a revolution (Zöllner 2009). By 24 September the demonstrations in Yangon had swelled to 100,000 people, led by tens of thousands of monks. The authorities called for the protests to stop, and when they did not, violence was used: starting on 26 September, smoke grenades, baton charges, rubber bullets and live rounds were deployed. That night many protesters, including monks, were arrested. By 1 October the SPDC brought the demonstrations under control. The authorities now focused on night raids and arrested thousands of those who had taken part, many of whom had been filmed in action. The detainees were held in makeshift detention centres around Yangon, interrogated and classified into different categories according to which they were either released or imprisoned. Although students were involved, they did not lead these protests. Rather, as seen in the following quote, they followed the monks. As Ma Phyo Phyo Aung (a former student leader of the All Burma Federation of Student Unions, cited in *University World News*) remarked, 'The difference between the 2007 Saffron Revolution and now [post-2021] is that there are protesters who are the younger generation and are leading the protest actively against this 2021 military coup' (Naw Say Phaw Waa 2021). 2007 was quite different from 1988 – and very different from 2021. After the protests had died down, the path towards the reforms and the elections continued unabated, as if nothing had happened.

The road map was long and drawn out, including the writing of a new constitution that paid lip service to the participation of different ethnic groups but did not actually heed any of their demands. Through its Constitution, the SPDC offered a change to a form of 'disciplined democracy', focusing on duties and responsibilities over rights and affordances (Metro 2017), while also framing proper moral conduct (Walton 2016). The Constitution made sure that the Tatmadaw would retain 25 per cent of seats in all legislative assemblies (Union, State and Region) as well as control over three key ministries (Home, Border and Military Affairs). Any changes to the Constitution would require more than 75 per cent of the vote of the Houses of Parliament, ensuring that the military would control any such changes. At the time of the referendum in 2008, just days after Myanmar had been hit by Cyclone Nargis causing thousands of deaths in the delta and Yangon, there was a significant movement against the Constitution, demanding democratic change rather than what the junta was offering. Students from the 88 movement led a campaign against the new constitution on the grounds that it did not include delegates from the NLD, and advocating for the release of political prisoners.[7] The SPDC took no notice of any of the dissent and made sure that the referendum passed. The 2008 Constitution paved the way for the preparation towards the first elections in 20 years. Held in November 2010, they were won effortlessly by the military party – the USDP. The new government was led by former General Thein Sein, who like Ne Win before him, had taken off his uniform to become a civilian leader.

Reforms

In 2012 President Thein Sein's government initiated a series of socio-economic reforms across all sectors. President Thein Sein had been chosen largely because of his lack of charisma and because he was not seen as the type of leader who would go beyond the window dressing of change that the junta envisaged. To everyone's surprise, he turned out to be a much stronger reformist than expected. He started by speaking to the wider population on the radio, laying out a programme that included national reconciliation with the NLD, a peace process with the ethnic armed organisations (EAOs), economic reforms and engagement with the outside world, as well as educational and social reforms. Step by step he made good on his word, inviting the 1988 activists back into the country, allowing free press, engaging with foreign donors as well as empowering local civil society to make unprecedented changes. In this period, Myanmar transformed at an astonishing speed. Lall's book on Myanmar's reform process (2016) details this period of radical change. The next section will focus on the educational reforms of this time – in particular those concerning higher education – and the politics behind the changes made. This period was key in forming the students who went on to protest after the 2021 coup d'état; it was also very important in transforming the way higher education was delivered and how institutions were understood in relation to the growth and change of the country.

Educational reforms

President Thein Sein's government developed a ten-point education plan that would form the basis of what was to come during his following five years in office. Unlike any of his predecessors, he saw a role both for local civil society and international development partners in Myanmar's development (Lall 2016). In February 2012 a Conference on Development Policy Options with Special Reference to the Health and Education Sectors was organised by the government and development partners. As a result of this conference, the Comprehensive Education Sector Review (CESR) was launched in July 2012. The CESR was spearheaded by the Ministry of Education and supported by a range of international development partners including the Asian Development Bank (ADB), UNICEF, and national aid agencies, such as the UK Department for International Development (DFID) and the Australian Agency for International Development (AusAID, now Department of Foreign Affairs and Trade [DFAT]). The CESR's responsibilities encompassed all sectors of teaching and learning – from early childhood education to higher education – and involved a wide range of ministries and departments with a stake in these areas. The focus of the CESR was on reviewing the formal state education sector around the country in four stages. After the first phase of work (entitled 'Rapid Assessment'), proposals under consideration for basic education included increasing basic education from 11 to 12 years and changing the teacher career structure – two major structural changes to which all other areas within education would have to adapt. The CESR completed its Phase 1 review in early 2013, followed by CESR Phase 2 (entitled 'In-Depth Analysis'), where more detailed work was conducted resulting in detailed reports for each of the education sectors. CESR Phases 1 and 2 provided a much clearer understanding of the status of the education sector, allowing the identification of recent achievements and priorities for continued reforms and investments. Phase 3 focused on the cost of implementing necessary changes across the sector for the years 2016 through 2020. This was followed by Phase 4 and the drafting of the National Education Sector Plan (NESP). This plan became the guiding document for the whole sector. It was later renamed the National Education Strategic Plan (NESP) but otherwise was broadly accepted in its original form by the National League for Democracy (NLD) government that took power after the 2015 elections (Lall 2016).

It is important to note that the CESR (2012–15) was research-based, and its lessons were the basis for the development of the NESP. The CESR included a lot of primary and secondary data research funded by donors and led by specialists and consultants, with a focus on good international practice. But there was also a significant amount of primary national research, often supported by retired and semi-retired officials who were involved in education committees or who had previously worked as academics in Myanmar's universities.[8] This research culture was new to Myanmar, and the involvement of academics and their research in policy work was quite 'revolutionary'. Since the NESP became the primary policy document for the Ministry of Education driving the reforms, it can be argued that in the initial years of reforms, the Ministry of Education experienced some evidence-based policy making with research at the heart of driving change. Unfortunately after 2016 there was little independent research conducted by the Ministry of Education; the ministry was overwhelmed with delivering the nine transformational shifts promised in the NESP. Research no longer drove the change process as data was no longer routinely collected to answer policy or research questions. This point is important because the reduction of research as a driver for change increased the gap between the policy makers and the affected population, resulting in some practices across the education sector that were not seen as particularly useful or adequate. Continued centralisation was also part of the problem since local issues could not be addressed at a local level. This was so because education in Myanmar is not a state/regional subject, so there was no decentralisation, and no real 'deconcentration'[9] at state and regional levels. All decisions were taken at the union level and state or regional governments and parliaments had no say in how education was delivered. The strict hierarchical nature of ministry business is another reason that the education reforms were unable to deliver the kind of transformation that had been envisioned at the start of the change process. Post-2015, ordinary people, especially outside of the urban areas, might have felt less affected by the reforms, fuelling the sense of general dissatisfaction that was, in the end, used as an excuse by the Tatmadaw to initiate the coup – as explained in the next chapter.

The National Education Law

The drafting of the National Education Law in 2014 was a landmark in the education reform process. The law attempted to address the key issues facing higher education in Myanmar, including the autonomy of universities, the right to form unions and the right of universities to formulate their own curriculum (Kamibeppu and Chao 2017). However, the law was not without controversy. Believing that it did not go far enough, student protests would rock the streets of Yangon and other cities in Myanmar in 2014. As the law was being discussed, momentum for protest increased; civil society organisations and student and teacher unions accused the government of excluding them and not taking advice from the relevant stakeholders into account. Those drafting the law were seen as not having a stake in Myanmar's higher education system, wanting rather to maintain a version of the 'command and control' system. The NNER, led by Dr Thein Lwin, held meetings that decried the law as cementing the centralisation of Myanmar's education system. The meetings resulted in a set of detailed suggestions that were submitted to Parliament. The main issues that had sparked unhappiness included the lack of teaching of ethnic languages and cultures at universities, the lack of independence afforded to universities and whether it was legal for students to take part in political activities. The Action Committee for Democratic Education (ACDE) – comprising members of the All Burma Federation of Students' Unions (ABFSU), the Confederation of University Student Unions and University Student Union – began to campaign for the amendment or redrafting of the National Education Law. Demanding a quadripartite meeting between ACDE, NNER, the Government and Parliament, they held a demonstration between 14 and 17 November 2014 at various locations in Yangon and other parts of the country and threatened nationwide demonstrations if the government did not respond within 60 days. Once the 60 days expired, more than 100 people started to march from Mandalay to Yangon – a 404-mile distance – commencing on 20 January 2015. Other protesters joined the march from across the country, including from Pakokku, the Delta, Dawei and Mawlamyine. The 11 points issued by the ACDE on 24 January demanded both a meeting with the government and for the law to be amended.[10] Some of the points were framed in terms of equity and social justice. This included the demand about equality for students with disabilities and the inclusion of ethnic languages in higher education so that ethnic students could more easily take part. Others focused more on issues of governance and autonomy, in particular the freedom to establish student and teacher unions, as well as the inclusion of teachers and students in higher education policy making.

In contrast to its response to previous protests, the Government agreed to meet with the students in February to discuss their demands. Three quadripartite meetings took place, during which time the student protests continued. As Dr Thein Lwin, a long-time supporter of Daw Aung San Suu Kyi, had been expelled from the NLD, the NLD was not seen to be on the side of the NNER and the students. This came as a shock to students, who could not understand why the NLD would not support them at such a crucial time. It also showed that the NLD would side with the government rather than the protesting students when it came to governance, centralisation and control issues. Students maintained that their protests would only stop after the new or amended law had been passed by the Parliament. At the last meeting, an agreement was struck, with the government promising to take into account the 11 demands. The government repeatedly asked the students to suspend their protests; even a head monk lent his support, requesting the students 'to go back to their studies'. However, tensions grew and when police tried to prevent the protesters from marching on to Yangon from Latpadan, the protests became violent. Solidarity protests by students and civil society organisations near Sule Pagoda in downtown Yangon were violently broken up by the police in March 2015. The government not only used police to control the protesters and manhandle them, but also employed civilian thugs, who were either recruited from poor areas or had recently been released from jail. The riots resulted in the arrest of 127 students and students being beaten in the streets. Ultimately, the contentious National Education Law was revised in 2015, but there were only minor concessions from the government, and it remained largely as it had been originally drafted. Metro (2016) argues that the National Education Law makes it clear that the three governments – the SPDC (1988–2010), the Thein Sein USDP-led government (2010–15) and the NLD-led government (2015 onwards) – had very similar conceptions of 'democratic education'. Each wanted to retain centralised control of higher education and HEIs, and the autonomy they promised was largely symbolic.

After the 2015 elections, the reforms were taken over by the newly elected NLD government. The National Education Strategic Plan (NESP) of 2016, launched by the NLD government in February 2017, was based almost entirely on the previous government's draft National Education Sector Plan (Lall 2021a). Buddhist principles remained embedded within the language and interpretation of the national legal framework and education policy did not change much. Despite the government being run by the NLD, students continued to protest when their views clashed with those of the government. This included protests against the University of Yangon centenary in 2019–20, which were seen as window dressing rather than meaningful reforms (Proserpio and Fiori 2022).[11]

Reforming higher education

Higher education remained a top priority of the NLD government. As the reforms were rolled out, the sector was poised for complete transformation. Even though wider education reforms had started in 2012 with the CESR, higher education had remained quite closed to external influence until 2016. Myanmar had much to catch up on, both compared to the rest of the region and globally, and international aid agencies were ready to step in. The appointment of Dr Myo Thein Gyi, the former rector of West Yangon University, as the Minister of Education in 2016 resulted in serious efforts towards delivering the priorities defined in the NESP, in particular in higher education.

The NESP (Ministry of Education 2016) identified three strategies for higher education reform based on the National Education Law and the CESR, namely: (1) to strengthen higher education governance and management capacity;[12] (2) to improve the quality and relevance of higher education; and (3) to expand equitable access to higher education. Whilst the NESP promised to allow universities to gradually become more autonomous, the biggest hurdle remained in the centralised government-controlled budget that did not allow individual institutions to make their own decisions. The granting of autonomy was tentatively tested when the University of Yangon and University of Mandalay were allowed to select their students and, as of 2020, permitted to hire some of their own staff.[13] As part of the broader reforms, undergraduate students were being reintegrated to the main campuses of urban universities. New government higher education coordinating bodies were created, such as the National Education Policy Commission[14] in 2011, the National Institute for Higher Education Development in 2017 and the Rectors Committee in 2018 (Lall 2021a). The Policy Commission was designed to have an executive role in advising and coordinating higher education policy and legislation in the form of Myanmar's 30-year Long-Term Education Development Plan, as well as coordinating with development partners (Channon 2017).

The higher education reforms were guided by three broad aspirations: (1) meeting Association of South-East Asian Nations (ASEAN) regional benchmarks for higher education; (2) gaining a place on the international league tables; and (3) the need for higher education and research to support post-conflict national development. The first two stem from a neoliberal discourse, influenced by international aid agencies and feelings of national pride, while the latter is based on notions of state-building (Kandiko Howson and Lall 2019).

A technical annex of the CESR cites Myanmar's desire to adopt ASEAN standards as benchmarks for its own reform higher education goals.[15] At the time, the state of Myanmar's higher education system compared unfavourably with its neighbours in the region in terms of investment in education, research output, knowledge economy indices and enrolment ratios. The CESR Phase 1 Report (2013) summarised the overriding aspiration for higher education as an improvement in 'systemic quality' that included employability, targeting the skills needs of the workplace, the expansion of the private sector and internationalisation. The need to approximate standards found elsewhere in ASEAN and internationally was explicitly recognised, as was the need for broader international collaborations and certification, resulting in the National Education Policy Commission starting to engage with the ASEAN standards framework. Part and parcel of this approach was research. Research was a headline in the NESP goals and at the centre of the nine transformational shifts, as such underpinning the entire reform process:

> Improved teaching and learning, vocational education and training, research and innovation leading to measurable improvements in student achievement in all schools and educational institutions. (Ministry of Education 2016, p. 12)

Research was also mentioned in the NESP Theory of Change (Ministry of Education 2016, p. 66) as well as part of a strategy to increase the decentralisation of education in order to improve quality of what is delivered:

> Therefore, the MOE will research, draft and launch a new national policy on decentralised decision making in schools and townships. This policy will provide a legal framework for the expansion of school grants to include school quality grants proposed under the Basic Education – Access, Quality and Inclusion chapter. (Ministry of Education 2016, p. 92)

Research featured most prominently in chapter 8 (on higher education), where it is was framed as a way to contribute to society and as an intrinsic part of the academic work to improve the quality of universities and their teaching.

At the time of the reforms, Ministry of Education officials started to express the wish to develop 'world-class higher education institutions' that could enter the global university rankings. Despite this sounding fanciful, the NLD actively sought help in the form of aid money and experts from both Britain and Australia to support the (re)development of the University of Yangon as a leading HEI. This was a personal priority of Daw Aung San Suu Kyi, who wanted to see her alma mater, the historical flagship University of Yangon, restored to its former 'glory' as one of Asia's leading universities (Esson and Wang 2018). There was little debate on how this unrealistic drive towards the league tables (Lall 2021b), likely at the expense of developing regional universities, would lead to an increased stratification of the system by exacerbating the urban/rural divide. However, this push had one positive consequence – the reintroduction of independent research into universities. In order to compete in international league tables, some flagship universities began to promote working towards international levels of research and publications. Research became increasingly important as changes were made to higher education governance. Although Myanmar academics had a long way to go to catch up with their regional and international peers, there was a broad understanding that only an improvement in research practice would lead to a wider improvement in teaching and assessment. The Department for Higher Education (DHE) established a database of university research. In an interview at the Ministry of Education in 2018, the DHE explained that HEIs were in control of their research whilst the DHE provided the research grants. Each year, the Director General explained, the DHE would decide how much funding they had to distribute for research. In 2018, for the first time, the Rectors Committee was involved in the grant allocation process. The process started with university rectors at each university selecting three to four research proposals from amongst their staff, which were then suggested to the Ministry for funding. At that time, all the proposed projects were funded for the first year, but longer projects had to be specifically selected in subsequent years for continued funding. This system was completely new and attracted great interest across universities. In 2018 the DPE received over 50 research proposals from arts and science universities, in addition to computer and technical university proposals. In an interview, one development agency representative mentioned that reforms were faster in the universities for agriculture, medicine and technology because their work was linked to economic development and their research fed into industry. This means the Ministry of Commerce was also supportive of this type of research. Education Colleges (ECs) that had been integrated into the higher education system were also funded to do research: each EC received 10 lakhs Myanmar Kyats (1 million) for action research that was to feed back into the ECs teacher training. Whilst the DHE at the Ministry of Education funded most of the university research, the Director General expressed hope that as universities became more adept at doing research and their institutional autonomy grew, they would also be able to apply for research funding elsewhere.

At the same time, research became a vital part of university promotion structure, with research publications becoming a requirement for those seeking advancement. The universities used research to monitor performance, and this became a key criterion in the 'service marks' category. The Director General explained that the Ministry looked at the number of research papers where the academic was first author (domestic and international publications being treated equally), followed by service to the institution and then the degree the academic had and where it was from. Promotion decisions started to take these categories into account rather than relying on seniority and years of service, as had been the case before. Research output increased; approximately half of research papers were published in international journals in 2018 (Ministry of Education 2020a), although research quality remained a concern, with certain papers plagiarised (Symaco and Hayden 2024). At the time of the research, there was no coherent research policy in Nay Pyi Taw either at the national or institutional level. The process of research feeding into policy would have taken some time; as one Ministry of Education respondent explained, *'the universities do the research, they write papers, but the results are kept in the university'*.

In supporting 11 universities during the reform process, UCL tried to support institutional frameworks that would underpin research, including helping the senior staff of these HEIs to conduct small research projects on their institutions (including, for example, researching the student experience at their university and exploring the creation of ethics committees). This kind of collaboration between elite universities from the Global North and Myanmar's HEIs was common and expanded quickly. The Ministry of Education reported 102 Memoranda of Understanding/Agreement with foreign institutions in 2014–15, falling to 51 and 29 in the subsequent two years (Ministry of Education 2019, p. 53, fig. 2.6.4). Universities had hoped that these collaborative arrangements would help their academics meet international standards; however, as noted by Heslop (2019), most Memoranda of Understanding were inactive and if they resulted in collaborative research, they tended to benefit the institution from the Global North. Heslop also observed that the neoliberal push for international collaboration with urban flagship universities would not help meet the local needs for higher education to promote integration and social justice across ethnic regions and conflict-affected regions within the country due to chronic underfunding of the sector (Heslop 2019). This issue of equity between Myanmar HEIs – especially between urban and rural locations – and across the higher education sector as a whole was a wider problem that had been recognised and needed to be addressed.

In a 2018 national Higher Education Conference, a Ministry of Education representative's presentation, *Equity in Myanmar's Higher Education: Opportunities and Challenges*, emphasised that equity was still a major priority of Myanmar's higher education reform. He held that increased disparity would widen the social divide, gradually leading to social unrest, conflict and chaos in society. Therefore 'equity interventions' were needed to reduce disparities and include marginalised groups, ensuring social justice and facilitating the social cohesion, peace and prosperity of society at large. He noted that one way forward was to establish more HEIs across the country to address the imbalanced distribution, reflected in too many students enrolling in low-quality distance education programmes. In fact, only 2.8 per cent of the aforementioned population 15 years old in rural areas had a university degree, compared to 16 per cent in urban areas. The urban/rural divide was also seen in the allocation of resources: regional universities had much higher teacher–student ratios than urban institutions, with a teacher–student ratio of 1:5 in Yangon University but 1:29 in Kalay University in the west. Unfortunately, these discussions remained at the policy rather than the implementation level.

Reaching its halfway point in the summer of 2019, a mid-term review (MTR) was undertaken to allow for a re-prioritisation and some streamlining of programmes within the Ministry of Education and to help draft NESP 2. The MTR final report explained that the reforms were complex and ambitious, because they involved many large-scale activities occurring simultaneously. The MTR stipulated that the education reforms still had a long way to go (Ministry of Education 2020a). NESP 2 (2021–30) was drawn up on the back of the MTR at the end of 2019 and beginning of 2020. Despite the recommendations made in the MTR, there was little consultation with the affected stakeholders. The Ministry of Education led most of the processes, with procedures not clearly explained to development partners, leading to some frustration. Before the NESP 2 drafts could be revised or finalised, COVID-19 interrupted the reforms.

Myanmar and COVID-19

Myanmar's first encounter with COVID-19 was more fortunate than that of many other countries. When the pandemic became a widespread threat in Southeast Asia in March 2020, Myanmar schools were about to start their year-end three-month holiday. Myanmar universities were more affected, as some were closed in the middle of their end of semester exams. In March 2020 the Ministry of Education decided to close all institutions with the intention of holding exams after the pandemic (Khaing Phyu Htut et al. 2022). It is reported that about 11.6 million learners enrolled for the 2019–20 academic year were impacted by this closure.

A COVID-19 Response and Recovery plan was developed (Ministry of Education 2020b) but it was not comprehensive. The plan did not, at first, expect a long pandemic and there were hopes that all education institutions (including HEIs) would resume as usual in June 2020. The plan also seemed to lack coordination. Most of the discussions were quite centralised within the Ministry and did not take stakeholder views into account. Several entities were involved in making decisions to do with reopening educational institutions. Chief among them was the Central COVID Committee, led by the Ministry of Health and Sports, which produced a 90-point check list, subsequently used by the Ministry of Education to check education institutions before reopening. When the pandemic seemed to wane in July 2020, the Ministry of Education attempted first to open some high schools, but many schools found it challenging to meet the criteria on the checklist. The attempt to open schools triggered an increase in the number of local transmissions of COVID-19, and all schools were closed again from early August. While the Ministry of Education made some effort to enable continued learning during the pandemic, for example, by setting up an educational TV channel airing school lessons for primary- and secondary-level students, and distributing recorded teacher training video lessons for teachers, nothing much was offered for university students and staff. Only ECs were supported – the Ministry of Education established the Myanmar Digital Education Platform (MDEP) to provide teacher training based on the reformed basic education curriculum. Yet online teaching remained a challenge due to the lack of training. As explained by two teacher educators in research conducted by Khaing Phyu Htut et al. (2022):[16]

> The Ministry of Education has not properly trained teacher educators for online teaching, so it took longer than necessary

> to teach online. As a result, student teachers have lost their right to study. Another is that professional development programmes for teacher educators are not as effective as face-to-face online switching. Lack of interest, lack of participation. (TE-TT)

> Because of the COVID pandemic, to our Teacher Educator sector, we faced the failure of implementing incoming plans. We did not get a chance to keep reforming teacher education. We, teacher educators, lost opportunities to attend programmes or projects for continuous professional development. For our student teachers, they also lost opportunities for continuously learning as we could not give and share with them teaching knowledge what they need to know. (TE-AM)

It was never made clear why HEIs were not the first to be reopened and why HEIs were not considered equal to schools by the MDEP. The higher education sector's lack of decentralisation and autonomy also played a role, as HEIs could have been allowed to arrange online learning, but the hierarchical structure of the Ministry of Education made this impossible. In addition, in areas where the spread of COVID was low (such as Kayah, Chin and Kachin States), the nationwide closures were applied without considering contextual differences. The end result was that all HEIs across the country had to remain closed, irrespective of infection numbers (Khaing Phyu Htut et al. 2022).[17]

'Reformed' higher education before the coup

Prior to the coup the higher education system included 174 universities under the jurisdiction of eight ministries. They fell into two broad categories: the arts and sciences universities and the technical and professional universities. Teacher education colleges had just come under the remit of the Ministry of Education as part of the education reforms. Private HEIs in Myanmar were still not permitted to identify themselves as universities, even if they were degree-awarding (Heslop 2019).

According to UNESCO data, the total tertiary level enrolment in Myanmar in 2018 was 932,901, of which 58.6 per cent of students were female (2021). The gross enrolment ratio was low, at just 16 per cent, largely due to a weak secondary school structure. There was little diversity in the tertiary sector, with most courses offered at the bachelor level. Only 3 per cent of tertiary enrolments were in the short cycle level and less than 2 per cent at the masters level, and only 2,785 enrolments at the doctoral level (Khaing Phyu Htut et al. 2022). Myanmar's distance education system had around 500,000 part-time students. Distance education (still) offers access for the poorer sections of society, as students can study part time whilst still working and living at home. In 2017–18, Myanmar had 13,610 teachers in higher education (Ministry of Education 2019). According to the government's Comprehensive Education Sector Review Team (2013), 83 per cent of academic staff and 60 per cent of students in 2012 were female.

Despite the decade of reforms, a main issue faced by the higher education sector at the time of the coup was the quality of teaching content and pedagogic methods; most academic teaching staff were not yet research active in an international sense and courses were being updated to meet international standards. The use of English as a teaching language remained a barrier to improved teaching and learning, because academic staff (as well as students) do not necessarily speak English well enough. Rote learning remained the norm, especially in universities outside of Yangon and Mandalay, where things had improved quite remarkably despite the resource crunch. The problems were compounded by the lack of modern information technology infrastructure, high teacher–student ratios and salaries that were deemed 'unattractive'. The system remained under-resourced and lacked specialised teaching spaces such as laboratories.

Elections leading to the coup

In November 2020 elections were held and the NLD won a landslide victory. Ministry of Education officials interviewed the year before were divided on how the education reform process would be affected by the 2020 elections. A number of them said that the elections had nothing to do with the Ministry of Education and that the ministry would plod on with delivering the NESP. Others disagreed, saying that the Minister of Education in particular would be under pressure. Most agreed that the CESR MTR results being so close to an election could have implications, as it would reflect on the success of the Ministry of Education: '*There will be political pressure on data interpretation*', '*The Elections will not affect the reforms, but the government will use the data for the elections to show the change*' (Ministry of Education respondent).

Conclusion and analysis

As has been seen, the education reforms quickly started to follow a neoliberal logic, copied mostly from Western donors. The issue of rankings and measurable quality factors were part of the daily discourse in the Ministry of Education. Recognising this shift from a state-led socialist logic of education to one that was more in line with the outside world is important. Myanmar universities were still stuck in the shell of colonial and socialist buildings that might not have resembled other global universities from the outside, but the reforms made sure that the Gramscian logic inside these buildings had started to change (Lall 2021a). Staff at the time of the reforms recognised the value of some of the changes, mostly with regard to greater autonomy and academic freedom. Not all were happy with the element of competition that started to rear its head. The small pots of funding that the Ministry of Education was making available to staff (described previously) were meant to encourage staff to compete with each other for research opportunities. Arguably, having some research funding rather than none – as had been the case previously – was a huge improvement. Staff did as they were told because that was how the system had always worked, and some certainly saw this as part and parcel of joining the international higher education 'order'. But the neoliberal logic underpinning this move, very much supported by the donors, was wholly alien to the traditional Myanmar way of thinking, and in private some staff voiced concerns.

Students did not agree with the neoliberal logic either. Despite benefitting from the wider freedoms, including those of speech and assembly, the vision for a reformed higher education in Myanmar was progressive. According to Proserpio (2025), 'throughout the reform period, student organisations actively embraced a more progressive and less neoliberal idea of HE and pushed for a more "just" higher education that could support a better, more inclusive society' (p. 121). Students started to organise themselves visibly in unions, not to overthrow the government, but rather to reform and reimagine their country through a better higher education system that would serve society and take for its basis the principles of inclusiveness and freedom (Proserpio and Fiori 2022). Already during the reform period, the students believed that universities were the key to social transformation and as such needed to be adequately funded and autonomous. As seen in this chapter, students were willing to go onto the streets to show the government what they believed was the right way forward in the reforms. Even when the authorities were fed up with the student demands and police used batons to beat the protesters or arrest them, their voices would not be silenced. As key stakeholders of the system, they demanded universities with adequate funds, governed with principles of inclusiveness and freedom, focusing on the idea that education should operate at the service of larger societal transformation, including working towards peace in ethnic states. The politics of Myanmar higher education were completely altered by the reforms, and students early on found a critical voice that united them, often pitching themselves against the reforming authorities. Lall's book on the Myanmar education reforms (2021a) argues that the NLD missed an historic opportunity to make the national education system more socially just and equal and that the desire of the ordinary academics, teachers and students was certainly for a reformed system, but one that reflected broader values, rather than those touted by the development partners who were financing the changes. As we shall see in the rest of this book, when the coup smashed the 'reformed' system, the revolutionary students made it clear that they would not want a return to the neoliberal logic. This is an important part of understanding the last part of the theoretical framework described in the Introduction and which will be elaborated on in Chapter 4.

The question of why the students protested is not difficult to answer. Throughout history and across many countries, universities have fermented dissent to authorities. From Japan (in the 1960s) to China (Tiananmen Square in 1989), from India and South Korea to the US, France and UK, universities have been bedrocks of movements of protest and dissent. Myanmar is no exception; if anything, the country has shown that, despite fierce repression, the student imaginary of a better world is inherited by each new generation. The main question here is why and how this youth-led movement has been able to sustain itself for four years after the coup, and why young people are still giving their lives for a better future. The answer lies in the reforms. Despite their neoliberal tone, the changes brought about a space where ordinary people and their children were able to hope for a better future.

Those students who were enrolled in universities at the time of the coup had spent their teenage years under the Thein Sein government, and therefore as teenagers and young adults had experienced Myanmar under reform (Lall 2021a). This was a very different Myanmar from the one their parents had lived in. It looked like the country was on the right trajectory. When the coup happened, the students rightly feared that recently granted freedoms would be taken away. The coup and the reaction of the higher education sector is discussed in the next chapter.

Notes

1 It was switched to Burmese under the Law of University Education of 1964. However, English was reintroduced in 1982 to recover the quality of education. This effort was not successful due to insufficient teaching materials in Burmese and staff facing difficulties teaching in a foreign language (Myat Thein 2004).

2 According to reports published by the Assistance Association for Political Prisoners (AAPP), before these months, the words 'democracy' and 'human rights' were rarely heard and even less widely understood in the country.

3 The estimated number of casualties differs widely but a death toll of 3,000 is the most credible estimate, with most of the victims being young people and students leading the demonstrations (Egreteau 2009).

4 While Lall (2016) clearly stated that democracy was *not* on offer and that a democratic system would *not* result from the reforms, many – including in the aid and development world – did not understand this. Many reports spoke promisingly about Myanmar's democratisation process. More recently, David Brenner (2022) critiqued the dominant framing of Myanmar's conflict as a fight for democracy, arguing that this lens overlooks deeper, historically rooted issues of state formation, ethnic nationalism and postcolonial legacies. His article calls for a shift from Eurocentric paradigms to localised understandings of conflict, rooted in Myanmar's own context.

5 Road Map to Democracy, see Lall (2016).

6 In October 2005 the regime had increased the price of both petrol and diesel by more than 900 per cent and basic commodities had gone up by 10–20 per cent within a week but there had been no reaction. The 2006 price hike meant that diesel went up from 1,500 to 3,000 kyat per imperial gallon and petrol from 1500 to 2500 kyat per gallon, while compressed natural gas (increasingly used by taxis, buses and for cooking) went up by 500 per cent. This time there were small protest marches, some involving a few leaders of the '88 Generation' student group. See Lall (2016) for details.

7 However, these were not large student-led protests. See PIME Asia News (2006).

8 JICA funded a Japanese professor to work at the Ministry of Education to support its staff in research practice.

9 Deconcentration is a form of decentralisation where there is little financial devolution but where regional level voices are taken into account.

10 The 11 points are:

- Inclusion of representatives of teachers and students in legislation process of education policies and laws, by-laws and other related laws
- The right to freely establish and operate student and teacher unions and legal recognition for them
- Establishment of National Education Commission and University Coordination Committee mentioned in the approved National Education Law
- Self-determination and self-management on educational affairs of individual state/regions and schools
- Modifying current examination and university matriculation system
- Modifying teaching methods to such that ensure freedom for thinking and self-studying of students
- Inclusion of a provision in National Education Law that ensures freedom for the practice of ethnic languages and mother tongue based multi-lingual education for ethnic populations and tribes
- Inclusive education for all children including children with disabilities
- Resumption of enrolment for students previously expelled from schools due to the student uprisings
- Allocation of 20 per cent of national budget for education
- Regulating of free compulsory education up to middle school level rather than primary level

11 Daw Aung San Suu Kyi had asked development partners to focus resources on the University of Yangon, her Alma Mater, to help restore it to its former glory. The resources spent on the University of Yangon were already disproportionate to those spent on other universities, in

particular universities located in more remote or conflict-affected States. Esson and Wang (2018) detail how money was wasted on decorative elements, rather than substantial changes, infuriating students.

12 Senior management teams (including rectors) from 11 universities (Myanmar's flagship university as well as three HEIs located in ethnic states) took part in a University College London-delivered Higher Education Leadership and Management Programme, set up in partnership with the Ministry of Education, the Irrawaddy Policy Exchange (IPE) and the British Council (BC). The co-designed programme was based on the NESP Intermediate Outcomes to help train the NIHED trainers and strengthen higher education governance and management capacity.

13 This, of course, is bound to create a difference between locally hired staff attached to individual universities and staff hired by the Ministry of Education, who rotate and have government employee status.

14 Called the National Education Committee (NEC) at the time.

15 Under the umbrella of the CESR Phase 1 Report, a technical annex on higher education was published in 2013 with a section entitled 'Summary and Recommendations' (p. vi), which contextualised Myanmar's higher education reform within the ASEAN region.

16 Please note that these quotations are taken from the jointly written article of Dr Khaing Phyu Htut, Prof Marie Lall and Prof Camille Kandiko Howson, as they illustrate the ravages of COVID on Myanmar's education sector. They therefore use different acronyms, referring to their jobs as Teacher Educators (TE) and the location of their institution. To maintain anonymity, no further details can be provided.

17 Some ethnic schools and colleges in Kachin and Mon States run by EAOs remained open during this time, showing that a decentralised approach could have worked.

2
Coup and reaction

> 'On one morning everything disappeared. Everything we knew disappeared.'

Introduction

The reforms described in the previous chapter resulted in some progress, notably towards Myanmar's work on reaching the Sustainable Development Goals (SDGs), something the international community used as a way of measuring the wider success of the reforms.

Measurable outcomes included the poverty rate falling from 40 to 30 per cent and per capita income rising by 50 per cent (2015–19); Myanmar moving up on the Human Development Index to position 145 out of 188; a reduction in the gender literacy gap; middle school enrolment in rural areas increasing; and chronic malnutrition of children falling from 35 to 29 per cent between 2010 and 2017. The Myanmar government even prepared the Myanmar Sustainable Development Plan 2018–30 to meet the SDGs.

Nevertheless, there were big differences between regions and states, urban and rural areas (Okamoto 2020). A 2019 review showed that with regard to education, literacy remained particularly low in Shan State (which accounts for 18 of the 19 townships countrywide), with more than half of children having never attended school. Mongkhet township was especially prominent: 85 per cent of its children had never attended school. Other townships with particularly high numbers of persons with no education were identified in Karen, Magway and Rakhine. Children from rural families and poor or otherwise disadvantaged groups were still less likely to transition from primary to secondary education, or to complete their secondary education. Health indicators showed wide geographic, ethnic and socio-economic disparities; infant mortality rates were highest in the districts of Labutta in Ayeyarwady and Mindat in Chin, whereas Magway, Sagaing and Tanintharyi had particularly high early years mortality rates. Children in rural areas were more likely to be chronically undernourished (32 per cent exhibiting stunted growth) than those in urban areas (20 per cent) (all figures from MIMU 2018). With regard to measurable outcomes, the reforms had brought about some progress, but there was certainly still a long way to go.

There was however one area where reform progress could not be measured; yet it turned out to be one of the major changes of Myanmar society and was about to become the most important indicator of the reform success – the desire for lasting change and the steady progress towards a participatory system where ordinary people enjoyed ordinary freedoms without being controlled by the military. There was a widespread desire for development and democracy and a belief that with the reforms, the country was on a path to achieve this in the future. The decade of change that the Myanmar people had lived through gave them hope, and for the first time – at least among young people in urban middle-class areas – a sense of having rights. When the future was taken away, there was shock, followed by anger and a sense that they had to fight back. Young people in particular felt a sense of responsibility. They did not want to end up like their parents, who had lived through the 1988 protests and despite their sacrifices had not seen the military regime removed. This time the fight had to remove the military from power and throw them out of the political process for good. As has already been mentioned, this book argues that it is because of the decade of reforms that the coup did not have the outcome that the Tatmadaw leadership had expected. This chapter describes the coup and the initial reaction to it in urban areas, in particular Yangon. It looks at the effects the coup had on the education sector, in particular higher education.

The coup

On 1 February 2021, Myanmar experienced its third coup d'état, putting an end to the decade of incomplete economic and social reforms described in Chapter 1. The Tatmadaw seized power from the NLD party one day before the new parliament was meant to convene – the NLD had just won the November 2020 elections by a landslide. The coup surprised most, as it was widely believed that even amid reforms, the Tatmadaw had retained its key role at the heart of government and had benefitted economically, politically and diplomatically from the reform process. General Min Aung Hlaing arrested the elected leader Aung San Suu Kyi, alleging electoral fraud.

The Asian Network for Free Elections (ANFREL), one of two accredited foreign election observer missions, expressed its opinion that the results of the 2020 general elections were, by and large, representative of the will of the people of Myanmar. As Philipp Annawitt (2021), who worked as an adviser to Myanmar's parliaments, put it:

> The coup [was] a nakedly desperate attempt by this clique of almost-has-beens to turn back the tide after the democratically-elected NLD government implemented an aggressively pro-market reform agenda that included mobilizing Western and East Asian investment into regular channels, improving public financial management and taking on corruption, which put the squeeze on the military's shadow empire.

These words resonate with the majority view of the over 50 million people living in Myanmar. In the same article, Annawitt (2021) added that 'the most important thing to understand about the coup leaders is that they are a clique of generals who control, through straw men, Myanmar's biggest corporations, as well as the lucrative trade in jade and other precious stones, narcotics and timber'. The Tatmadaw's vision for the country is epitomised in a militarised view of Burmanisation, with the military, as the country's largely Bamar elite, controlling the rest of society (Lall 2021a). The opening of the country through the reforms had brought to the fore critical voices of this vision, not least across the higher education sector, and this challenge had to be put down with force.

The international community reacted with horror and condemnation. Support for the reforms stopped as no more funds were to be transferred to the government now controlled by the Tatmadaw, renamed State Administration Council (SAC). Those in charge do not seem to have been too concerned; the SAC publicly announced that 'We [SAC] have to learn to walk with only a few friends'.[1] Few friends here meant China and Russia, who have a close relationship with the Myanmar military but who had not supported the wider reforms.

Myanmar's reaction to the coup

Protests against the coup started early in February 2021, only a few days after it had occurred. Initially, these amounted to a few lone protestors with a megaphone standing in a public place in Mandalay, while the rest of the nation digested the events in shock (Kyaw Ye Lynn 2021). Many of the demonstrators were quickly arrested, though some, like Dr Ko Tayzar San, managed to get away (Htet Htet Eindra Aung 2024). It looked at first as if the SAC's gamble had paid off: the streets remained deserted. Then things began to change. Protests erupted, led by doctors, nurses and students from government hospitals, which also include Myanmar's medical schools. As in 1962 and 1988, students were at the forefront of the 2021 revolt – although across the country many other groups joined the demonstrations, including many government teachers who presented themselves in their uniforms with the Ministry of Education's green flag.

Over the next few weeks the resistance coalesced around different groups, comprising members of Gen Z (those under 24 years old at the time), the 88 Generation, the NLD (and the National Unity Government they created) and the Civil Disobedience Movement (CDM). A sense of intergenerational solidarity quickly emerged, as those who had lived through the 1988 and 1990 protests saw these renewed protests as a continuation of their own struggle. However, it became apparent over time that Gen Z viewed their protests quite differently. While collaborating with the older generations of the other groups, they made it clear that their resistance would not settle (as had happened before). It is because of this drive that the protests and the resistance movement that started in 2021 are quite distinct from the kinds of demonstrations that Myanmar had experienced previously. As will be seen in later chapters, what started in February 2021 would engulf the whole country in a fierce war of resistance. But at the start, the different groups resisted in their own distinctive ways, and there was little coordination across those in defiance of the regime.

The education sector was mainly involved in CDM, whereby staff walked off the job and institutions had to shut. Those who refused to return to work were suspended or dismissed. The Ministry of Education also lost staff to CDM, although a number of senior staff stayed in place, implicitly accepting the new order. The Ministry of Education issued a circular stating that promotions would be denied to those who had taken part in the CDM. Staff were asked to declare whether they supported the protests and to identify those who did (Naw Say Phaw Waa 2021).

Because higher education staff are government employees, protesting academics were expelled from campus housing. In urban areas, the newly arrived Tatmadaw light infantry divisions (which are usually stationed in ethnic conflict areas) took over campuses as well as government hospitals to accommodate their soldiers. Teaching was suspended, mirroring the situation in the 1980s and 1990s, when universities were closed for over a decade and a half and a whole generation of young people missed out on higher education.

While universities and medical schools in particular took the lead in the protests and CDM, closely followed by health workers and civil servants including teachers, Narai (2022) argues that the massive general strikes on 22 February and 8 March were successful because of the participation of the members of the working classes, such as garment workers, railway workers and nurses, whose acts of civil disobedience paralysed the country. Resistance came in many forms – public protests such as marches and rallies, civil disobedience including walkouts and refusing to pay taxes, general strikes and the nightly banging of pots and pans. Egreteau (2022a, p. 822) describes these different forms of protests in detail:

> … set to the tune of a classic slow rock song by the American band Kansas, *Dust in the Wind* (1977), a Burmese-language song played incessantly through car stereos and loudspeakers, or sung acapella by groups of protesters, young and old alike. For many Burmese, *Kabar Ma Kyay Bu* (whose longer title roughly translates as 'there will be no pardon until the earth ends') is a revolutionary anthem, a battle cry that was composed during a previous uprising in 1988. It is a protest song that has since embodied resistance to military rule and repression. But in 2021, it was also sung with people raising their hand in a three-fingered salute.

The first street protests resembled a carnival. Placards made fun of Chief of Staff General Min Aung Hlaing, young people donned costumes. Most of those taking part in protest did so with their colleagues (with many university faculties, students and staff protesting together in their uniforms, or factory workers protesting displaying their union symbol). Egreteau (2022a) argues that this resembled the 1988 protests, in which people protested together according to their social networks. The slogan '*Doh-a-yay! Doh-a-yay!*' ('Our cause! Our cause!'), used in anti-regime riots before, resonated across the marching crowds.

In a response to the masculine military power on display protesters hung up women's longyis (*htamein*) as well as underwear. As tradition and superstition have it, walking under women's garments can take a man's masculine power away. The washing lines of women's clothing did make the troops deployed in Yangon uncomfortable – police and soldiers tried to remove the garments from the washing lines with poles and sticks before walking on those streets (Kuhakan 2021). Khin Khin Mra and Jenny Hedström (2024) describe how women also used protest tactics like bras and sanitary pads to confront military patriarchy. The role of women in the Revolution has become a major theme of academic interest (see Marlar and Chambers 2023), with Hedström et al. (2023) explaining how women have emerged as leaders of the resistance, with female garment workers and teachers spearheading early demonstrations. As they note in their 2023 article, women made up approximately 60 per cent of participants in CDM, and organisations such as Women's Alliance Burma coordinated actions across sectors and regions. Nyein Chan May (2023) argues that feminism became a big part of the protests, with the role of women key to resistance. Her analysis points to a shift in the attitude of young people regarding the role of women in Myanmar society, arguing that the coup brought about a greater sense of inclusion and equality between the sexes as the resistance grew. Greater inclusion and equality would also be on display with regard to ethnic and religious divides as the resistance to the coup evolved – but this took more time. The fact that young women immediately joined young men on the streets – and were treated by their peers as equals – was seen as unprecedented in Myanmar, where gender norms still play an important part in social relations. More of the shifts in attitudes regarding ethnicity and religion will be discussed in later chapters.[2]

Aside from the marches there were also general and silent strikes. Going beyond CDM, people boycotted state goods and activities, aiming to damage the economy and with it the SAC. At 8 p.m., families used the banging of pots and pans to express their dismay; cars, buses and trucks honked. Egreteau reminds us that this form of loud protest was also used in 1989 (*Far Eastern Economic Review* 22 June 1989, discussed in Egreteau 2022a).

For the first few days the regime forces – mainly the police – just stood there with shields. Protesters tried to talk with the police on occasion, trying to explain their position, asking them to switch sides (Nachemson 2021). The violence grew incrementally – first water cannon and tear gas, then sound grenades and rubber bullets. When the protests were met with increasing violence, the protesters set up barricades made up of whatever they could find including burning tyres to block the streets (Egreteau 2022a). The internet played a big role, offering lessons from other anti-government protests movements – such as the *#MilkTeaAlliance*. The three-finger salute from the Hunger Games, used in the Thai protests not long before, became a rallying symbol (Banki 2021). Protesters learnt online how the Hong Kong protesters had protected themselves from the tear gas. Students went into the protests with shields, masks and goggles – often not enough to be protected from the tear gas, and certainly not enough to protect them from the live bullets that started to be used by the military. It was the arrival of light infantry divisions that changed the nature of protests, as soldiers fired live bullets into unarmed crowds and snipers shot individuals in the head. The first killed was 20-year-old Mya Thwate Thwate Khaing, who participated in a mass protest on 9 February 2021 in Myanmar's capital, Nay Pyi Taw. Her death 10 days later was followed by thousands more fatalities as live rounds were used regularly against the protestors.[3] Volunteer medical teams were also targeted by soldiers when they tried to help the wounded, and many doctors went into hiding. Most hospitals and their medical schools remained closed. Mobile clinics were manned by medical students administering first aid to the wounded protesters. In one case captured on video, SAC security forces ferociously beat medics they had arrested with the butts of their guns, showing that even doctors were no longer respected, as they were seen to support the protesters (DW News 2021). Armed forces likewise responded to the nightly banging by shooting at the balconies where the protesters stood. In one widely shared video at the time, a female Yangon resident shouts out to the armed police or military that her family had always supported the Tatmadaw, but that the shooting was stupid and had caused them to lose all support. Over the next few weeks, the non-violent protests were supressed by means of brutal crackdown, arrests, torture and killings. Protesters and NLD politicians were tortured to death (Simpson and Farrelly 2021). Families were sometimes called to retrieve the bodies of those taken away the previous night, and in a number of cases, were asked to pay for the bodies of their relatives. There is no official tally of the number of students who were killed, but both the Assistance Association for Political Prisoners (AAPP) and independent reports indicate that young people and children constituted a significant proportion of the at least 6,337 civilians who were reported killed and 2,614 wounded for political reasons in the first 20 months after the coup in Myanmar (Min Zaw Oo and Tønnesson 2023).

The SAC, governed by General Min Aung Hlaing, also intensified the repression of both the CDM and protesters through a list of wanted people that included many academic staff and student leaders. It was read out on television every night at 8 pm, followed by nightly arrests. Those arrested included Australian academic Dr Sean Turnell, who was Daw Aung San Suu Kyi's economic adviser. Student leaders went into hiding, and some young people started to flee to border areas. But the Tatmadaw began to escalate the conflict in ethnic areas as well, and in March 2021 carried out the first aerial bombings in Karen and Kachin States in two decades.[4] Mobile and wireless internet were cut to make communication between protesters harder and all nongovernment media was officially shut down. Journalists risked their lives to report.

In the end, as the military meted out violence, many young people decided to counter the SAC in an armed revolt. As in the late 1980s and 1990s, they left for the border to join up with the EAOs, in particular the Karen National Union (KNU), to get armed training. Some remained within the structures of the EAOs, other created their own PDFs, discussed in more detail in a later chapter. The ousted parliamentarians who had not been arrested formed the National Unity Government (NUG) in April 2021. They endorsed the creation of the PDFs and the use of violence against the regime, proclaiming a 'nationwide defensive war' (Egreteau 2022a).[5]

Possible reasons for the coup

So why did the military leadership destroy a system that they themselves had created, that they were able to control and that had brought them international and even domestic legitimacy? The hybrid military–civilian model had brought global recognition and greater economic opportunities (Simpson and Farrelly 2023). Even as news had emerged from Myanmar that communication between Daw Aung San Suu Kyi and General Min Aung Hlaing had broken down, no one had seriously believed a coup was likely because the Tatmadaw itself had so much to lose. The claim of a 'stolen election' seemed so far-fetched (and so similar to Trump's claim in the US) that it was completely derided.

Although we will never know what exactly happened in the heads of those who decided to overthrow the governance structure they had themselves created on the morning of 1 February, it is fair to believe that the system was not working for them. The result of the 2020 elections in particular (with the NLD's landslide victory) had shown that the first past the post voting system did not work for the military's USDP, and that the military erroneously believed they commanded a sufficient level of support across the country that would be reflected at the ballot box. Ingrid Jordt (2021) discusses how the rivalry between Daw Aung San Suu Kyi and military leader Min Aung Hlaing was also deeply personal – the success of the former at the ballot box in 2020 clearly showed whom the electorate supported. Min Aung Hlaing's alleged desire to become president (since he faced mandatory retirement in July 2021), reportedly rejected by Daw Aung San Suu Kyi, meant that his path to power was blocked. As Jordt (2021, p. 5) observed, 'The move humiliated the General ... He was politically, personally, and financially cornered. The only path forward was to revoke democracy and presume the path of a world conquering king.'

But as always the truth is likely far more complicated – it is worth considering some other possible reasons for the coup. One was Min Aung Hlaing's belief that the broader Myanmar population was disillusioned with the NLD governance and preferred a Thein Sein-like government, similar to the one that had brought in the hugely popular reforms between 2011 and 2015. Some in the top brass believed that there was widespread discontent across the Myanmar people, compounded by the isolation that the COVID pandemic had brought. This was the first explanation widely discussed as it was linked to the accusation of voting fraud and ballot box stuffing. In urban areas there was genuine critique of the NLD's governance and the slowing down of the reforms. Freedom of the press and of expression did allow genuine discontent, compounded by COVID-19, to be voiced, especially on social media. As in all reform processes there were winners and losers, and the increased levels of poverty and urban economic disparities fuelled discontent. This, however, did not mean a desire to return to a military-led government.

General Min Aung Hlaing and his advisers' main error was to misunderstand the reasons for the grumbling across the country. The cause of discontent with the reforms – namely, that they were too slow in bringing change – was not the kind of dissatisfaction that called for renewed military rule. The resounding victory of the NLD in 2020 clearly demonstrated that the Myanmar people trusted the NLD to continue with Myanmar's transformation process, even if not all were satisfied with everything the government was or was not doing. Continued talk about constitutional change amongst the NLD members of parliament would not have helped, but in essence it was the lack of respect shown by the NLD when called to meet the Chief of Staff to discuss what he claimed was 'irregular voting' that ultimately resulted in the reaction that led to the coup. The system had been set up in such a way that the civilian government still had to listen to the military leadership and show the Tatmadaw due respect. The fact that they did not think this was necessary probably toppled the apple cart. In the end, it was the desire of one general who wanted to be president and could not fathom retirement in mid-2021 that led to the unravelling of the system.

Whilst there are some who argue that General Min Aung Hlaing and his acolytes were afraid of constitutional change, this was constitutionally impossible. It is more likely – as argued previously – that they saw the shift in attitude of some of the political elites (in particular the NLD vis-à-vis the armed forces, sidelining them in the political process) as the first step in the 'wrong direction'. There are also those that question the effectiveness of the military-engendered reform process and whether this transition was 'real' (Prasse-Freeman and Ko Kabya 2021). However, the reaction to the coup shows, if anything, that the reforms had been very real and had had a tangible effect on the wider population. The partial freedoms that the Myanmar people had finally enjoyed paved the way to a political consciousness. The opening up of Myanmar as a country led to access to technology and the creation of civil society networks (see Lall 2016) that all played an important part in creating the post-coup resistance.

The subsequent chapters show that Min Aung Hlaing's plan to take a step back and try to recreate a government similar to the one run by President Thein Sein between 2011 and 2015 backfired spectacularly. As has been argued by others, including Simpson and Farrelly (2023), the Myanmar people had experienced increased political freedoms and would not accept these being taken away by renewed military rule. The SAC's expectation that people would accept them taking back control did not materialise – on the contrary, it resulted in the kind of resistance that the Tatmadaw had never faced previously. The way that the opposition organised themselves, first to fight back peacefully and then with force, has surprised the military leadership. As documented by all those who write on Myanmar, there had always been resistance to the military. Different ethnic armed groups fought many different wars with the regime, and in the 1960s, 1980s and 1990s, students did as well. A complete revolution unfolding across the entirety of the country, was, however, unprecedented. The standoff that exists between the two sides at the time of writing means that it is impossible to imagine any form of 'peaceful co-existence between military and civilian rule for the foreseeable future' (Simpson and Farrelly 2023, p. 2).

The consequences of the coup for higher education

In May 2021 around 19,500 higher education staff were suspended. This represents around 55 per cent of academic staff.[6] Staff were asked to officially declare whether they supported the protests and to identify those who did. Some key CDM staff were punished by demotion or by being sent to more remote universities. The Ministry of Education issued a circular stating that promotions would be denied to those taking part in CDM. Because higher education staff are government employees, protesting academics were expelled from campus housing.

The government announced that postgraduate and final year undergraduate teaching would resume in May 2021, but given that most staff refused to work and universities were now army barracks, it was unclear how this would be feasible. All other undergraduate teaching was suspended, mirroring the situation of the 1980s and 1990s, that resulted in an entire generation being denied a higher education. In an article co-authored by Marie Lall (Khaing Phyu Htut et al. 2022), Yangon-based academics were asked about their reactions to the coup. Some of the quotes are reproduced here – allowing their voices to be heard:

> First, it stopped all the progress the higher education is having both in its management system and in its academic research. Second, students cannot have the continuous education via online programme that was being planned during the COVID before [the] Coup. Third, many good teachers give up their spots as they no longer believe in the education system operated by the military.[7] (HE-PP)

The first part of the respondent's reaction points to the fact that the reforms were completely undone overnight and that the students would suffer as they would not be able to continue their education. Even during the COVID period, there had been some sort of continuation, but the military takeover brought everything to a shuddering halt as teachers left their jobs.

> Disastrous! Over 90 per cent [of] students and almost 40 per cent (initially almost 80 per cent) [of] teachers and staffs joined CDM, boycotting the junta, saying bye to their universities as long as they are under the junta's control. Some teachers and students try to carry on education in all means possible but the majority cannot. (HE-YNSN)

This academic reiterates how the coup resulted in academics leaving their jobs to show their disagreement with the coup, resulting in the destruction of the higher education system. This is also the main point for the following respondent:

> [The] [c]oup affected the HE [system] seriously. Many staff have participated in [the] CDM to protest it. As a result, some have … hidden themselves in places where they cannot be known, or some cannot go to international universities to pursue further studies, which has negatively effects [sic] not only for themselves but also on the HE [system]. (HE-KTDM)

Not only academics, but also teachers were at the forefront of the protests and teacher education, that had just been integrated into Myanmar higher education, was also badly affected.

> The coup affected the teacher education sector negatively and seriously because those who are in the middle of the coup and who accepted it keep leading the teacher education sector. There would be no bright future because of those people who could not determine which is right or wrong and would like to encourage the bad people. (TE-AM)

As this quote indicates, teachers and teacher educators see a moral choice between remaining in their position – and being part of a military system – or walking away in protest. The CDM engulfed the whole education sector – as described in the following quote.

> Because of the coup, [a] CDM has developed. Many teachers and students participated in [the] CDM and were involved in the Revolution. So formal learning opportunities for student–teacher had been destroyed by the coup and teacher educators lost their jobs. Before the coup, we were going to implement the four-year new curriculum and upgrading Education Colleges to Education Degree Colleges, and all our plans have been destroyed by the coup. (TE-MP)

This quote echoes Proserpio and Fiori (2022), who explain that those working at universities were afraid the reforms would be stopped and reversed and that teachers involved in CDM did not want to lose the benefits they had gained, including the freedom that came with research.

As detailed by Ei Khine et al. (2024) CDM encompassed all sorts of people, ranging from those who were not at all politically minded to those who saw the higher education system as a political force. There were many different motivations to join – paramount was the desire to reverse the coup and the belief that joint action would topple the SAC. Their respondents described the coup as unjust, and even as going against the 2008 Myanmar Constitution.

This respondent quoted in Khaing Phyu Htut et al. (2022) also reiterates how the coup destroyed the progress made during the reforms. The following quote expresses the despair that many felt as their trust was broken.

> The main reason is that student teachers are losing their right to study. Some have given their lives in opposition to the dictator. Some have committed suicide due to mental illness. CDM teacher educators have been wrongfully arrested by the dictatorial military council. There were also killings. The trust between the teacher and the student; Respect and value. Understandings were ruined by a group of dictators. (TE-TT)

This last quote also reminds us of the cost of resistance: people arrested or killed for their belief in a better future for Myanmar. It also reflects the voices collected by Ei Khine et al. (2024) who detail the violence, humiliation at the hand of authorities, arrest and loss of their jobs which had often come with housing benefits. One of their respondents describes life on the run after her students were arrested, having to change location frequently and changing her name on social media. Others describe how their relatives were targeted by the regime after they had fled. There are also those whose families disagree with their position and their commitment to the CDM movement comes at tremendous personal cost when family relationships break. Lastly, the respondents quoted by Ei Khine et al. (2024) describe the difficulty in surviving without an income. Some have tried to open small businesses since they cannot be hired if they are a part of CDM. The quotes reproduced above and those collected by others indicate the deep chasm between the views of the academic and wider educational community and those of the military when it comes to the country's future and how it should be governed.

Post-coup health, education and higher education

CDM-affected medical schools and hospitals did not operate normally; one third of lead staff had left their positions. This in turn affected rates of COVID-19 immunisation and the care of the critically ill, especially during the third wave of the pandemic in the summer of 2021. Childhood immunisations (polio, diphtheria, measles) were disrupted, HIV and tuberculosis programmes reduced or closed because of lack of medicines or staff or both. The suspension of international NGOs such as Médecins Sans Frontières (in June 2021) means that, at the time of writing, the most vulnerable no longer had access to medical care. Other aid and development agencies also departed, many due to security concerns, leaving their programmes unfinished. As will be mentioned, medical schools have by now largely recovered because studying medicine is so prestigious for Myanmar families. Nevertheless, state health and education provision look very different after the coup.

It is challenging to access official data on schooling and university attendance at the time of writing. For basic education, which covers the grades up to the end of high school, there were reports that roughly 90 per cent of eligible students did not return to public schools when they reopened in June 2021 (Myanmar Now 2021). But non-enrolment rates have recovered somewhat, decreasing from 69.2 per cent in 2017 to 56.8 per cent in 2023 (World Bank 2023). For higher education, the general enrolment rate was 15 per cent in 2017, which dropped to 13 per cent in 2023.[8] As of 2023 about 28 per cent of 6–17-year-old children are out of school (compared to 21 per cent in 2017). As the number of out-of-school children increased, the per-student expenditure for households has also grown; it has become more expensive for children to go to school (World Bank 2023). According to an interview with an education specialist at FCDO in Yangon in 2022, before the coup, 9.8 million children were in school. After the coup, enrolment fell to 5.2 million, with actual attendance at 4.2 million; the matriculation (exam taken before leaving high school) was usually taken by around 900,000 students annually before the coup. In 2022 total attendance in all three grades of high school was around 362,372, indicating that very few will finish high school. There was also a reduction in the number of operational schools. Because of the CDM, only around 290,000 out of the 450,000 teachers previously working in Myanmar have returned to service.

However, the parental boycott of education has waned in the three years after the coup. Parents have been threatened by the authorities, but the lack of options and high levels of poverty means that many families have no choice but to send their children to government schools. There has been a form of normalisation in certain urban areas. According to a report by the World Bank (2024), the enrolment rate at primary level has now surpassed pre-pandemic levels (with a 27 per cent increase between 2023 and 2024), while the increase at secondary level was 28 per cent between 2023 and 2024.[9] However, regions such as Chin and Sagaing, which are the areas affected by the armed conflict, show very low enrolment rates, reflecting significant population displacement (World Bank 2024).[10]

While people have returned to work where possible, many have lost their jobs or opted to leave the public sector. The interviews with students on the border revealed that many of their parents had decided to open small shops to survive rather than remain in an employment linked to the SAC, even if that meant much less revenue. The chaos in the banking sector and the plummeting of the Myanmar currency, combined with rampant inflation, means many are experiencing hardship and the poorer segments of society have been facing hunger (UNDP 2024; World Bank 2024). The poverty rate reached in 49.7 per cent in 2023 (up from 24.8 per cent in 2017) and an additional 25 per cent of the population is barely above the poverty line. Moreover, 28 per cent of households report eating less as a coping strategy (UNDP 2025). Economic hardship is more acute for internally displaced persons (IDPs) who have to depend on casual work or humanitarian assistance (World Bank 2024). This means that for many families, education has become a lesser concern; making sure that there is food on the table is the top priority.

In higher education, CDM resulted in the dismissal/suspension of 50 per cent of academic staff, who also lost their housing. The ministry endeavoured to replace academic staff with junior staff – lecturers were promoted to professor and up to 3,000 new tutors/demonstrators were hired. In an unofficial post-coup interview with a Ministry of Education official, it became clear that the main issue the Ministry of Education was facing was the training of the new staff. Universities reopened when the spread of COVID-19 abated around July/August 2021. At that time, only first-year students attended. Later a second cohort started and anecdotal evidence started to emerge that the reduction of staff numbers due to CDM was affecting the quality of teaching. The new staff, recruited after the coup, were both less experienced and less competent.

According to colleagues inside Myanmar, the student enrolment rate in the first year is higher at professional universities, such as medical, dental and other medical associated universities, than at arts and science or distance learning universities. After the coup, the medical university first-year enrolment rate quickly rose back to around 90 per cent. At the time of writing it is unclear whether other subjects offered at urban SAC HEIs have recruited their usual numbers of students and if these students are attending in person. This showed that the boycott of SAC-controlled educational institutions is no longer comprehensive. In fact, the World Bank report claims that tertiary enrolment had also increased by 25 per cent between 2023 and 2024. The report attributes this to a sense of urgency to get education, although it could also be a way of avoiding conscription, as students are granted a temporary reprieve from being drafted.

Since the coup, universities in Myanmar have returned to the way they operated before the decade of reforms. The SAC reversed the higher education reforms by bringing back old policies and hierarchical structures. Universities that were inching towards limited levels of autonomy have had any decision-making powers taken away from them again. The Ministry of Education is responsible for the curriculum and academics who work at state universities are obliged to follow the Ministry's orders. Colleagues who decided to remain in their posts and who agreed to speak anonymously and informally about the changes reported being under scrutiny. They stated that they had to be careful about what they said and whom they spoke to. They also reported being careful in their interactions with students and in what they taught in class. This reflects the situation from before the reforms, when there was a climate of fear across universities and academics felt oppressed. The benefits of academic freedom gained during the reforms have been lost (Khaing Phyu Htut et al. 2022; Proserpio and Fiori 2022).

In the picture that emerges, education not only ranks high among the sectors most impacted by the 2021 military coup and its aftermath, but – to a greater extent than at any time in Myanmar's history – the education sector itself has become a battlefield. This becomes clear when looking at the displaced students' activism, which has resulted in the creation of alternative HEIs – discussed in Chapters 3 and 4.

It is important to note that in conflict-affected areas things can look quite different depending on whether the SAC, an EAO or a PDF is in charge of the area – and control and governance on the ground keep shifting. IDPs have established schools within their camps; however, they face several common challenges. Dropout rates are three times higher for displaced families compared to those households that have not experienced forced migration. And the enrolment gap between IDPs and non-displaced children is two times higher in rural areas (World Bank 2024). Financial constraints often hinder IDP families' ability to adequately support CDM teachers resulting in reduced incentives that may affect teachers' commitment.[11] Additionally, schools frequently lack essential facilities, equipment and infrastructure (such as desks, toilets and access to water). There is also a significant shortage of teaching materials, including printers, which are necessary for producing the textbooks provided by the NUG Ministry of Education in digital file formats. These factors collectively diminish children's enthusiasm for studying, leading to higher dropout rates. It may lead students to choose to join a PDF instead of continuing their education.[12]

Post-coup international assistance

The 2021 coup in Myanmar has completely reversed the landscape of international aid, bringing it back to its pre-2011 state. More precisely, the aid landscape has returned to that of the era of military rule under the SPDC, when development assistance ceased, leaving only humanitarian aid.

During the military regime from 1988 to 2011, most countries and multilateral donors suspended official development assistance (ODA) to Myanmar. After the Tatmadaw shot down the student protests in 1988, Western nations took a firm and uncompromising stance against the junta, imposing economic sanctions and limiting assistance to strictly humanitarian support.[13] Japan, historically the largest provider of overseas development aid (ODA) to Myanmar, also restricted its assistance to technical assistance, grassroots initiatives and human resource development (Kudo 2024). Consequently, China became the sole provider of large-scale infrastructure assistance (Kudo 2008; O'Connor 2011). Cyclone Nargis in 2008 significantly increased the humanitarian aid Myanmar received, although compared with the responses to other natural disasters, the amounts remained relatively modest.[14] The international funds were nevertheless significant. They allowed civil society organisations to deliver assistance directly to the Delta and as a result strengthened the civil society networks that would become a key force in the reforms that followed (Lall 2016).

A pivotal shift occurred with the national reconciliation between Daw Aung San Suu Kyi and President Thein Sein's government, transforming Myanmar from a recipient of solely humanitarian aid to one eligible for broad-based development assistance across economic and social sectors. This political transition positioned Myanmar as Asia's 'last frontier' for donor countries, NGOs and multilateral organisations, including the

World Bank. As sanctions were lifted during the political transition, donor agencies expanded their presence, and international aid surged within a short period, reflecting Myanmar's new-found status as a favoured aid recipient (Rieffel and Fox 2013; Fumagalli 2022; Kudo 2024).[15]

Japan, for example, not only provided large-scale debt cancellation and rescheduling for arrears accumulated since the socialist era, but it also facilitated a bridging loan to clear Myanmar's debt with the World Bank and the Asian Development Bank. Additionally, Japan initiated the Thilawa Special Economic Zone near Yangon through public–private partnerships (Kudo 2024). Similarly, US bilateral aid to Myanmar increased significantly, particularly after the NDL assumed power in 2016, targeting democracy, peacebuilding, human rights, food security, disaster prevention and health (Rizky 2021). The EU also expanded its assistance for peacebuilding, trade, rural development and governance. As was discussed in Chapter 1, education was one of the key sectors that benefitted from this surge in international aid. The influx of educational assistance supported HEIs and research collaborations, fostering a new generation of professionals and policymakers.

However, the 2021 coup abruptly halted this 'development aid boom'. The World Bank and other multilateral organisations immediately suspended new disbursements, and most donor countries ceased financing new projects while imposing sanctions on military-linked entities and individuals.

Aid has since shifted to the humanitarian sector. The United States redirected funding to support civil society and initiatives aimed at restoring democracy (Rizky 2021), many of which are located on the border with Thailand. The EU explicitly stated that its aid would be limited to humanitarian assistance delivered through local organisations, focusing on food security, nutrition, sanitation and shelter (European Commission n.d., 'Myanmar/Burma'). Japan suspended new ODA projects after the coup but continued those agreed upon before the coup, including the industrial zone project. However, new projects focus solely on humanitarian assistance, mostly provided through multilateral organisations (International Cooperation Bureau, Ministry of Foreign Affairs of Japan 2023).

There has been a focus on education aid, and scholarship programmes have become a prioritised channel for supporting Myanmar's people post-coup. The United States introduced several scholarship opportunities for Myanmar students. In addition to the longstanding Lincoln Scholarship for master's students, the Diversity, Equity, and Inclusion (DEI) Scholarship was launched in March 2024, specifically targeting marginalised communities. However, this initiative was abruptly suspended in early February 2025 under the Trump administration (RFA Burmese 2025a). The EU launched the European Union Mobility Programme for Myanmar (EMPM), a pilot scholarship initiative for students who were forced to suspend their higher education after 2020, enabling them to resume studies at universities in ASEAN countries through physical attendance or virtual learning. In its pilot phase between 2023 and 2025, EMPM allowed 83 students (across three batches) to travel to other ASEAN countries to complete their studies. Japan has historically supported the training of public servants since 2002 through the Japanese Grant Aid for Human Resource Development Scholarship (JDS). Myanmar had sent the second-largest number of public servants to Japan under this programme between 2002 to 2019 (Kudo 2024). However, with the official suspension of new ODA, training for civil servants under the SAC administration became politically untenable. Instead, since 2024/5, Japan has redirected its efforts to providing scholarships to those from the private sector through the Myanmar–Japan Center for Human Resource Development (MJC).[16]

Conclusion and analysis

The results of the coup led first to a complete breakdown of state services including education and health. The brutal crackdown resulted in many fleeing – there are no official statistics on the number of students that have left the country. However, as of late November 2024, according to UN estimates, around 3.5 million people have been internally displaced inside Myanmar (UN High Commissioner for Refugees 2024). Moreover, since the coup it is estimated that at least 1.2 million have fled outside the country, where they have joined pre-existing refugee and migrant populations. The precise extent of displacement is unknown but reports from civil society suggest that the true figures could be much higher.

For a few months, urban resistance resulted in targeted bombings of state buildings (such as township offices or schools) and assassinations of officials. Pro-military mobs also started to use explosives against those known to be critical of the SAC. The military ramped up its counterinsurgency campaign, previously focused on EAOs, to include the rapidly increasing number of PDFs. The conflict started to spread across the country. Not only the border regions, but also Bamar areas such as Sagaing and Magwe quickly came under fire, whilst fierce battles raged in the Kayah, Karen and Chin States, where students had fled to join the resistance. The Tatmadaw switched to aerial bombings wherever they suspected anti-regime forces to be present. This was a new tactic that had emerged during the reform period, when the Tatmadaw had used some of the available time and money to modernise its air force. Certain EAOs in Shan State and in Rakhine used the ongoing conflict and expanding theatre of war to increase the territory under their control. Figure 2.1 shows how EAOs and PDFs have gained control over large parts of the country (Henschke et al. 2024).

As discussed by Simpson and Farrelly (2023), by the end of 2021 the entire country found itself in the midst of a new civil war – battles raged everywhere and no one was spared. At first, the SAC fought the urban resistance with mass arrests, and torture. In 2022 four anti-coup activists were executed (Coppel 2022). At the time of writing, other death sentences are still pending. The young people who had fled the urban centres created militia forces (PDFs), some of which aligned themselves with the opposition NUG. The war moved out of the urban areas to ethnic states on the border and spread across the Bamar heartlands. More on how the PDFs have been resisting the regime is in the next chapter. The NUG endorsed the violence against the SAC as a war of liberation; neither side has shown any willingness to negotiate and both are intent on the eradication of the other. The revolutionary forces – be they the NUG, the PDFs, the EAOs, the CDM movement or the students conducting the Revolution through education – all agree that the Revolution has to remove the Tatmadaw from politics completely and once and for all, no matter the price, in this war which has engulfed all parts of the country. The war escalated further as the SAC activated the conscription law, making those young people who had hoped to sit out the crisis at home flee for their lives (Danish Immigration Service 2024). This has swelled the ranks of the armed and unarmed resistance.[17] The suggestion by the SAC in the autumn of 2024 that elections could help resolve the impasse and their invitation to EAOs to form political parties have been met with derision, hardening the resolve of many involved in the anti-regime fight.

Returning to the theoretical framework introduced in the Introduction, it is clear that at this stage of the Revolution we are dealing with a youth social movement as depicted in Novelli et al. (2024), reflecting the Foucault–Habermas lens (on steroids). This youth-led movement was largely made up of university students, but it also encompassed other members of Gen Z, some of whom were still in school and others already working. The identity of those still in school merged with those at university – and they are included when the term 'student' is used in this book. Others did not identify with the student label, which is why when

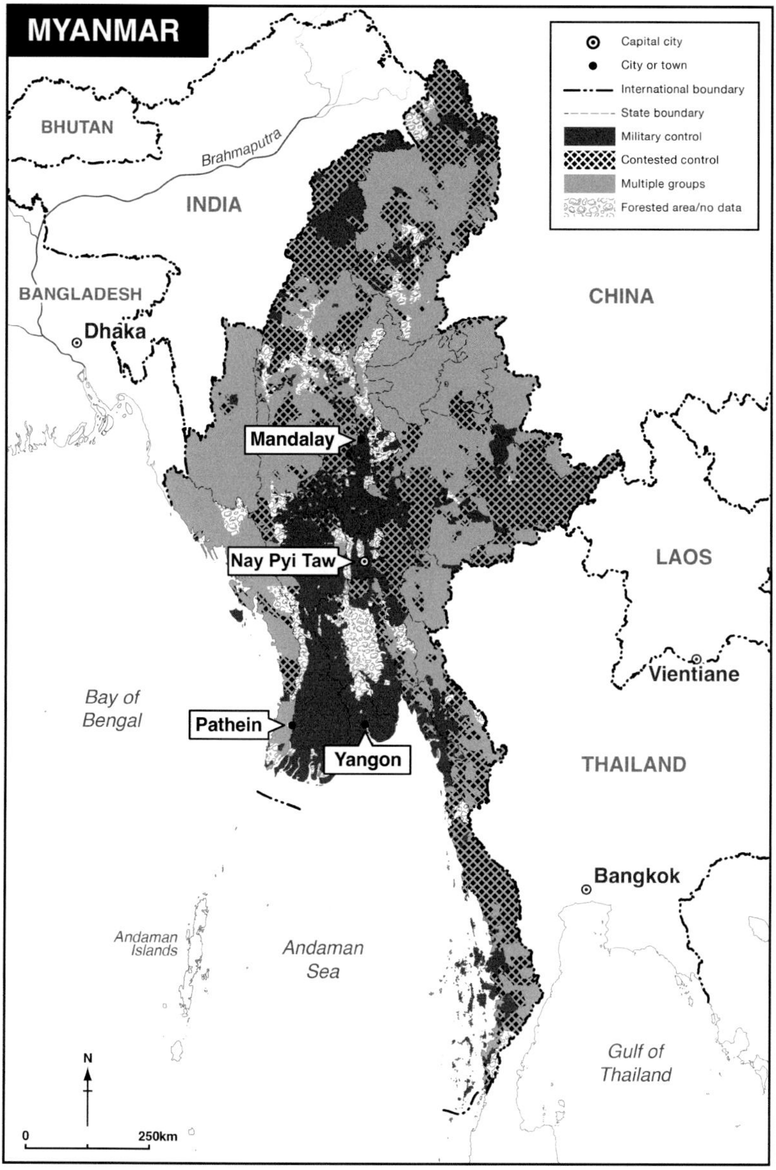

Figure 2.1 Map showing territorial control in Myanmar. Prepared by Miles Irving using OpenStreetMap. © Authors.

this book refers to the wider Gen Z protests, the term *youth-led* movement is used. Whatever the occupation of its participants, what matters is the collective anti-SAC identity that has emerged and forms the backbone of the movement (Tin Maung Htwe 2023).

The youth-led protests went beyond marching in the streets; leaderless networks emerged, modelled after the Hong Kong and Thai protests (Jordt et al. 2021). As such, the Myanmar protests have to be understood as a reflection of the Gen Z imaginary of the Global South, quite different from the kinds of protests that had happened in 1988 and 1990, arguably more shaped by Western ideas. The inspiration and the knowledge that the protesting Myanmar youth drew on came from both their own neighbourhoods and the innovative practices that had been used on the streets of Bangkok and Hong Kong. Social media served as a wide space for debate and knowledge making – both in a practical sense (e.g., learning how to manage tear gas attacks by the military) and more theoretically (in terms of the debates about the future of the country). The protests became a space for 'public pedagogy' (Khin Oo Thazin 2021). Tin Maung Htwe (2023) shows how student unions engaged in both political and civic education, bridging formal academic spaces, and Khin Oo Thazin (2021), using examples of the garment workers' strikes and the creative '*htamein*' protests, reframes street protests as educational spaces where values of democracy and equality are taught, highlighting its role in generating collective learning, identity formation and democratic praxis. These examples reflect Novelli et al.'s (2024) 'laboratories of learning' where new ideas were experimented with. While the protests had started simply to try to force the SAC to recognise and respect the election results and free the NLD leaders who had been arrested, the debate quickly changed to one in which youth were protesting for the complete removal of the military from politics. How this developed further will be discussed in the next chapter.

Notes

1 https://www.channelnewsasia.com/news/asia/myanmar-coup-activists-vow-more-protests-after-38-killed-14329382 (webpage no longer available).

2 But it has also become apparent that as the resistance movement has grown and taken up arms, there is increasing gender-based violence against women, especially in the PDFs (anonymous interview with Myanmar researcher in Tokyo).

3 See Tin Maung Htwe (2023), who focuses on the role of student unions and youth networks in the Spring Revolution to show how young activists adapted strategies, built coalitions with other societal actors and used digital media to sustain resistance against the junta.

4 Aerial bombings have continued. See Head (2023).

5 See also Pedersen (2023), who explains that the emergence of the NUG and the broader resistance movement – including armed and unarmed actors – marks a radical departure from past anti-military strategies. This generation of pro-democracy activists is more grassroots-oriented and more diverse. Beyond fighting the SAC they seek to dismantle the centralist, Bamar-dominated model of governance.

6 This figure is from the Myanmar's Teacher's Federation. For basic education, the number is 125,900, accounting for 31 per cent of all staff.

7 Please note that these quotes are taken from the jointly written article of Dr Khaing Phyu Htut, Prof. Marie Lall and Prof. Camille Kandiko Howson, as they illustrate the early effects of the coup on Myanmar's education sector. They therefore use different acronyms, which refer to their jobs as Higher Education Teachers (HE) or Teacher Educators (TE) and the location of their institution. To maintain anonymity, no more details can be provided.

8 The largest decline of NER was at the high school level.

9 This would need further investigation on the ground. Over-age students catching up on education loss due to the pandemic and the coup may be one reason.

10 The young people living close to the border with India had a different experience from those who had fled from Myanmar's urban areas to the Thai border. The large-scale destruction of towns and villages through aerial bombardments (in particular in Chin State) meant that many fled across the border to India for safety. We do not document their experiences in much detail, but India's contradictory policies with regard to Myanmar affected refugees are notable. More on India's policies is provided in Sarma and Kapur (2021).

11 Whereas this book focuses primarily on the experience of students, the journeys and challenges faced by CDM teachers are depicted in Jirattikorn (2023). See also Nyan Lynn Thit Analytica (2022a), who discusses the gap between promises of financial and logistical aid and actual delivery, contributing to attrition among participants.

12 Interview with a CDM teacher in a refugee camp in India.

13 In reality – because of the sanctions – there was hardly any humanitarian support apart from what Japan was providing, with only UNICEF active on the ground. Myanmar received a fraction of the humanitarian support Laos or Cambodia were receiving at the same time. Things only began to shift after Cyclone Nargis in 2008.

14 Around $300 million (Deutsche Presse Agentur 2009).

15 This trend had a negative impact on the humanitarian organisation operating in the borderlands, as the fund was for use within the country rather than on the border.

16 MJC was established as a JICA project to enhance human resource development, targeting the private sector, in 2013.

17 The social issues this has created are discussed in Chapter 4 and the Epilogue.

3

Resistance and Revolution: Gen Z student experiences and identities

> 'People are participating in the Spring Revolution in three ways: through Civil Disobedience Movements, strikes and armed revolution, each contributing as much as they can. Despite facing significant challenges, the entire country remains actively engaged in the Revolution.'

According to a 2022 report on the impact of the coup and conflict on education, over 1.1 million people were displaced initially, with children and young people facing disruptions to learning and heightened protection risks (Global Education Cluster and Child Protection AoR 2022). This chapter sets out to describe the Gen Z young people who were not only affected by the coup but who also responded to it. As explained in the Introduction, the focus of this chapter is on students rather than the wider group of young people who are a part of the resistance. The aim of this chapter is to discuss how they describe their identities in light of the dramatic political change, their sense of purpose after the coup and the different forms of resistance they have chosen to engage with. An important part of the picture is their new environment and the challenges they face in surviving, many on the Thai–Myanmar border. The chapter will also discuss some of the migrant support services that have been trying to help these students but whose capacity is insufficient, especially because of the large numbers of young people fleeing Myanmar.

Who are the revolutionary students outside Myanmar?

Most students across the country joined the protests in some form or another. Given the social media coverage and the photos available to all across the various online platforms, the SAC was able to identify rather quickly who was involved. Respondents explained that the list of students, even if they were not activists or leaders of the protest movement, is comprehensive. Any student who had taken part in any of the protests would not be able to leave the country legally and would most likely be detained at Yangon airport – which is why so many students decided to cross the border illegally, using brokers.

Many students fled to EAO areas or joined the PDFs to actively resist the coup. In this case they received combat and explosives training (more on their forms of resistance follows). Some of those on the border had taken up arms and served on the front lines, but either due to injury or exhaustion had ended up in Thailand.

The respondents on the Thai–Myanmar border have different backstories and experiences, but all of them actively took part in the protests and therefore had to flee because of their political engagement. The main difference between students is what level or lack of legal status they have in Thailand. Most students who fled Myanmar and crossed the Thai border are without any form of ID whatsoever. Many left in a rush, pursued by the police. The Thai authorities do not recognise them as refugees; Thailand has not signed the international refugee convention and refers to the waves of Myanmar refugees as IDPs although they have crossed an international border. There is some form of registration with UNHCR, but only very few have had any kind of support from the UN agencies.[1] Only a limited number are eligible for the third-country settlement scheme under UNHCR and with the huge pile of pending applications they need to wait under uncertain conditions for a long time. This scheme also seems to limit its engagement to high-profile refugees rather than helping the broad masses who fled across the border.

It seems that a small number of students managed to leave legally with their passports, receiving an entry stamp upon their arrival in Thailand. These respondents were all middle class, had left rather early in the protests, often urged by their families to 'get out', and were generally receiving regular financial support from their families inside Myanmar. Many of them have enrolled at Thai universities and restarted their studies from scratch. However, most of the respondents for this book left with only with their Myanmar ID – that is, the Myanmar National Registration Card (NRC), which does not guarantee any status once they are in Thailand. They are stuck in Thailand, as they are unable to apply for a Myanmar passport because of their political activity. Some respondents explained that with a Myanmar NRC in a fake name, it was sometimes possible to get a passport, but it was risky.

To ensure a level of safety and stability in Thailand, some students have attempted to obtain Thai migrant or worker ID papers, often through illegal means. The easiest and cheapest option is the 'police card', which requires a monthly fee of 400 Thai Baht to be paid to the police. This card is issued by the Mae Sot police authority and valid only in Mae Sot.[2] If opportunities arise and they can afford it, the students aim to obtain a 'pink card' which functions as a de facto work permit, at least in Mae Sot.[3] The 'pink card' offers stronger identification and broader coverage compared to the police card. Among the respondent students, 30 out of 56 held a 'police card', while 15 had a 'pink card'. Additionally, one student each had a *Tambon* card, border pass, or UNHCR registration, while eight students did not possess any of these IDs.[4]

Beyond their legal status, there are differences between these students based on their location and their family background. Most of those who have made it to Chiang Mai (more likely to have some form of ID, mostly passport holders) are middle class. Even in Mae Sot there are a select few whose family are middle class and able to send them money; but most living on the border are not only undocumented but have no financial help and have to find ways to survive on their own. This often means that they have to work for Thai employers who take advantage of their vulnerable status. Students joked that they had to 'hire' their employer by paying them, rather than receiving a salary themselves.

The students who completed the survey (56 in total) crossed the border between 2021 and 2023, signifying that there is continuous outflow of students from Myanmar. Out of 56 students, 31 were male, indicating no specific gender imbalance. Most of the respondents were either Bamar or of mixed Bamar origins (39 out of 56), while the others were from Mon, Karen, Dawei, Shan, Pao and Rakhine backgrounds. Most of the students were Buddhist (42 out of 56). Their ages ranged from 15 to 27 years old. Among them, 41 were studying in or had completed an undergraduate programme, while 15 were either about to enrol in university or were still in high school before moving to Mae Sot. Their family backgrounds were diverse, with households engaged in a variety of occupations (such as public and parliamentary service, commerce and business, factory or mechanical work, teaching, farming and engineering). As discussed in the following section on Myanmar students inside Myanmar, parents have also changed jobs after the coup to avoid working for SAC institutions. This means that some families that would have been considered lower middle class prior to the coup would now be considered working class.

Refugee students – both those who took the survey and many others who spoke to us in interviews and FGDs – are the main protagonists of this book because of the way they have decided to engage with the Revolution. Many have chosen to resist the SAC with their minds rather than their bodies, although some of the respondents had fought on the front lines before coming to the border. As will be seen across this volume, the work they do to support the resistance goes beyond picking up a gun. They say that they do not want to 'waste' this coup. Rather, they see it as definite turning point that can rally the whole country behind an agenda for change. Yet for this change to last, they believe that a comprehensive mindset shift is required and that education is, therefore, the key to lasting transformation. Their voices deserve to be heard, not least because of the sacrifices they are making every day for their country.

Whilst this book will focus on their voices, there are other stories that are also part of this Revolution, such as the experiences of those who decided to stay in Myanmar – as discussed subsequently.[5]

Students who stayed inside Myanmar

Not everyone crossed the border into Thailand. Those who stayed in Myanmar and did not join the resistance in the jungle or on the border fall roughly into two categories. The first of these includes students and families who refuse to have anything to do with SAC institutions, maintaining an internal boycott. Despite the economic hardship, even poor families joined the protests and others became poor because they joined the CDM and lost their jobs and housing. Some did not continue to protest because of family economic hardship and the need to keep earning money to put food on the table. In general, students from rural or remote areas, but also those in poor urban outskirts, come from very poor families. If they are students, they often are enrolled in the (very poor quality) distance universities that allow them to work whilst studying for a degree. The economic situation in Myanmar at the time of COVID and after the coup has meant that many young people have to work, even whilst studying.

There is anecdotal evidence that families who refused to continue working in government employment, even if they did not come out to protest, switched their occupation to run small shops or small businesses, eking out a living in the private sector. Young people from such families have started to work to help support their families. If they want to continue their studies their only option is to enrol in one of the Spring Universities described in the next chapter. This can be difficult: to access these internet sites a VPN is needed, and VPNs are illegal, there are electricity blackouts and the whole family is put at risk of arrest.

Not all students protested – regardless of their personal views, the second category comprises those who stayed at home. Some did not join the protests because their parents kept them at home (remembering the risks they had faced in 1988), others because they genuinely are not politically active and were waiting for the storm to pass. While students who did not join the protests can rejoin SAC-run universities, it is a difficult choice. Eighteen months after the coup, the boycott was already no longer comprehensive. Universities reopened when the spread of COVID-19 abated around July/August 2021. At that time, only first-year students attended. Then there was a second cohort, followed by more regular intake. CDM academics had been replaced by junior staff and there is anecdotal evidence that the reduction of staff numbers due to CDM is affecting the teaching. The newly recruited staff since the coup are less experienced and less competent. Nevertheless, universities are open, classes are being taught, and as seen in the previous chapter, the number of enrolled students is rising.

According to colleagues inside Myanmar, the parents spoken to say that the student enrolment rate in the first year is higher at professional universities – medical and medicine-related universities, dental universities and technology-related HEIs – than at distance learning universities and universities focused on the arts and science. As has been mentioned, the medical university first-year enrolment rate quickly recovered to around 90 per cent after the coup. At the time of writing it is unclear what other subjects are offered at urban SAC-controlled HEIs. Students and their families might not admit publicly that they have made the choice to get on with their lives for fear of social ostracism by those who continue to support the CDM. And some re-enrolled students decided to do much of their studying at home. Nevertheless, certain universities were starting to fill up again.[6]

It is no surprise that there are stark differences based on students' location. Students in urban areas have more options with regard to returning to university and more options for accessing alternative learning platforms, especially if they are from middle-class families. Student located in rural areas have less space to hide; depending on who controls the area they live in (SAC/ PDFs/ EAOs) they might not have much choice regarding a return to their studies. Some students who had been studying in Kalay, a border town between Chin and Sagaing, returned to their hometowns along the Myanmar–Indian border when their university closed down due to COVID-19. Because of the worsening conditions in Kalay, they never returned to university. One student, who had been attending college in Haka (Chin State), decided not to return due to pressure from fellow students to join the CDM, despite his hopes of continuing his studies. Another, who was in his second year of engineering studies, had led student demonstrations in Kalay and was also a member of the Kalay PDF for two months. He lived with his family in the town until early 2024. However, as the situation in Kalay deteriorated, he decided to go into hiding in a remote village, leaving his family behind.[7]

Respondents also described 'hybrid areas' where control switches between the Tatmadaw and the PDFs, or where the Tatmadaw controls the urban areas and the PDFs the rural villages. Students in these zones have to move to Tatmadaw-controlled areas to access the internet, which involves substantial risks. Students in areas close to the border might also have access to EAO post-secondary provision, which are generally not degree bearing. No data was directly collected about EAO post-secondary education provision, but as this sector has grown since the coup it will be discussed in the next chapter.

Forms of resistance

Resistance to the coup falls into several categories. Most visible is the armed resistance in which young people have used their bodies to fight the regime. Then there is the intellectual resistance, where young people decided to resist with their minds.[8] This book focuses on the latter. Nevertheless, since so many students joined the armed resistance, some information is provided here before the chapter reverts to describing the students who joined the Revolution without taking up arms.

The young people who fled to the border to get arms and explosive training from the EAOs soon started to form units of their own, calling themselves the PDF. Such PDFs increased quickly in size and numbers.[9] There is not much information available about their experience, apart from what former fighters disclosed in the FGDs after crossing the border into Thailand. However, given that so many young people joined the armed resistance, this section provides some background on how the PDFs operate as part of the wider Revolution.

The NUG did not create the PDFs but tried to unite them under the NUG flag as a coordinated response to the coup, 'taking control' of the emerging forces on 5 May 2021. The NUG's attempt to integrate the PDFs and coordinate the military response under a centralised command has been moderately successful; there are, however, plenty of PDF groups that have remained outside the NUG fold. PDFs are not homogeneous – as a term it encompasses regular military units as well as smaller units such as the Local Defence Forces (LDFs) that were originally formed to protect protesters, and the People's Defence Teams (PaKhaPha/PDTs) that operate as self-defence and guerrilla units at a community level (Ye Myo Hein 2022; United States Institute of Peace 2022). In 2022 United States Institute of Peace (USIP) estimated that there were at least 30,000 LDF personnel ranging from a dozen to a few thousand per group, mostly operating at township level and relying on homemade weapons. Their focus is on disrupting the SAC's administrative control, especially in rural areas, by using landmines, sabotage and targeted killings (United States Institute of Peace 2022). The PDTs are another version of the PDFs based at village level. They are generally more closely aligned with the NUG and specialise in urban guerrilla warfare, often also helping to train new resistance fighters. According to the NUG, PDTs have been formed in 250 out of 330 townships, mainly in central Myanmar, including the Sagaing and Magwe regions. Although they are primarily equipped with homemade small arms, they are an essential link between communities and the wider resistance.[10]

The Centralised Military Command structure (C3C), jointly led by the NUG and some EAO allies, came into being in October 2021. The EAOs that are affiliated with the C3C are the Kachin Independence Army (KIA), the Karenni National Progressive Party (KNPP), the Chin National Front (CNF) as well as the All Burma Students' Democratic Front (ABSDF). The KNU has remained outside of the C3C, but a Joint Command and Coordination (J2C) has been created with the NUG to coordinate operations held in the KNU-controlled areas (United States Institute of Peace 2022). In 2022 the PDFs comprised around 65,000 troops (United States Institute of Peace 2022). Some of them, such as the Chinland Defence Force (CDF), Karenni National Defence Force (KNDF) and Kachin People's Defence Force (KPDF), operate under the C3C but are not otherwise aligned with the NUG. Most PDFs work under the Military Division Commands (MDCs), which are semi-autonomous. MDC1 covers Kachin, Central Myanmar and Chin with 200 PDF units, 50 PDF units operate under MDC2 and three in Karen and Karenni.

The PDFs in ethnic areas are under the command of the local EAO.[11] As the 2024 International Crisis Group (ICG 2024a) report explains, ethnicity plays a big role in both the structure of resistance and the fragmentation of the state. The ethnic side of the resistance equation cannot really be separated out of the revolutionary narrative as the Karen, Kachin, Karenni and Chin EAOs sheltered activists and politicians from central Myanmar and provided military training. According to Brenner (2024), even EAOs that have not officially aligned with the NUG have proven instrumental in forming, sustaining and escalating the war against the junta. The EAOs' objective has been – for many decades before the coup – to end the Bamar political supremacy and to establish a federal state that would give the ethnic regions significant autonomy to manage their own affairs. Many EAOs have governance structures including schools (Lall 2021a) and justice systems (Kyed 2020), which they do not want to give up. As such, their aims differ from the Bamar PDFs who are fighting for the removal of the Tatmadaw from politics and the establishment of a democratic system of government.[12] It is this drive that has brought the conflict to Myanmar's heartland – it is no longer focused on the borders, where the EAOs have been fighting for decades. Their motivation, a desire to change Myanmar's governance and political system, is what unites both EAOs and PDFs, even if their vision for a post-Revolution Myanmar might differ significantly. Many EAOs are more concerned with consolidating power in their own ethnic homelands than mounting a united national offensive; diverging goals have created new challenges for resisting and destroying the SAC.

According to Brenner (2024), ethnic and revolutionary priorities came together in two cases when revolutionary movements forms in ethnic nationality communities, separately from the original EAOs. The CDF and KNDF have created student movements based on their ethnic marginalisation, but ultimately seeking a complete change of Myanmar's political system.[13] Their two areas have historically had less powerful EAOs. According to Brenner (2024), 'Chin and Karenni revolutionaries are not only fighting for a change of political system, but for the remaking of Myanmar's nation-state itself' as they are aware that any democratic system that maintains the traditional ethnic structures 'will not address their structural marginalization notwithstanding who is in power'.

Against a backdrop of decades of ethnic marginalisation, it would seem logical for EAOs and other ethnic organisations to join the revolutionary movement to bring down the SAC. And whilst the Karen, Kachin, Karenni and Chin EAOs broadly aligned themselves with the NUG and the wider movement, other EAOs and ethnic organisations did not. Paul Vrieze (2023) observes that not all EAOs have been supportive of the resistance; in particular, those associated with ethnic parties have been sceptical of the NLD. The role of ethnic organisations in the Revolution is beyond the scope of this book, but the differing views across EAOs and ethnic society, some of whom (as detailed earlier) see the Revolution as a fight between Bamars, is important as it affects the support received by the PDFs.[14]

As the Revolution has progressed, the PDFs have grown in size, organisation and capability.[15] At the time of writing, battle-hardened troops pose a real threat to the SAC despite their lack of heavy equipment (United States Institute of Peace 2022). Their tactical ingenuity and resilience has meant that the SAC has had to implement conscription to supplement its troops. Their advances are detailed in Shona Loong's six warscapes (Loong 2022).

But armed resistance is not the only way to counter the coup, and battles are certainly not enough to give rise to the future that revolutionaries envisage for their country. Whilst the PDFs need to defeat the Tatmadaw in the field, there is also a need to rethink and re-envision what Myanmar will look like if the Revolution is successful. The student identity and its purpose in this context is the subject of the rest of this chapter.

Student identities and purpose

Identifying as a student has been, in itself, a way of resisting the regime. This is not new; student protests in the 1960s, 1980s and 1990s were described in Chapter 1. Being a student was central to the identities of respondents from 17 different Myanmar universities (Table 3.1), all of whom explained that it was paramount that they continue studying.

Table 3.1 Universities of the students who responded.

Serial Number	Name of University	Number of Students
1	Dagon University	6
2	Mawlamyaine University	5
3	Distance University	4
4	University of Yangon	3
5	Thanlyn Technology University	3
6	East Yangon University	3
7	University of Economics Yangon	2
8	Paan University	2
9	West Yangon University	1
10	Magway University	1
11	University of Medicine Yangon	1
12	University of Medical Technology	1
13	University of Nursing Yangon	1
14	Yadanabon Cyber University	1

Table 3.1 (continued)

Serial Number	Name of University	Number of Students
15	Hinthada Technology University	1
16	Kyaukse Technology University	1
17	Magway Technology University	1
18	Not Available	4
	Total	41

Source: Authors.

Note: The above figures exclude 15 high school students and graduates who were also among the responding students.

The critical need to continue studying

Being a student, remaining a student, finishing a degree or at least continuing to learn new things was a key issue for the students on the border. Their views might differ from those who have taken up arms and joined the PDFs or EAOs to fight on the front line. It must be noted that the research for this book did not include interviews with serving soldiers, only those who had left their units once injured or exhausted to recuperate on the border. It is therefore unclear whether these students would see the continuation of their studies in the same way as those who took part in this research. What is clear is that those who did make it across, and those inside Myanmar who were interviewed via the survey, all saw their identity, their future and the future of their country tied to studying for a degree. As the quotations in Chapter 5 will show, they believe that Myanmar needs educated people to navigate through the Revolution and beyond. So most continued studying in some form – whatever they could manage. Courses they were accessing mostly online included languages such as English, Chinese, Korean and Japanese; knitting; programming; animation and research skills. Others were preparing for the General Educational Development test (GED) at Migrant Learning Centres or had joined courses at the 'Spring Universities' – more on this subsequently and in the next chapter.[16]

The lack of having money or the ability to earn it, described in more detail subsequently, is a barrier to be able to continue studying. Before the coup, being poor in Myanmar was less of an obstacle to accessing higher education than it is now, both inside and outside the country. The students who have reached Thailand and who have the financial means have enrolled in Thai universities. In certain cases, when not yet enrolled at a university, they prepare for the GED examination in order to be allowed to enrol. In all cases they have had to start from scratch. As will be detailed, since the coup, the migrant learning centres (MLCs) that had been offering education for migrant children on the border have increasingly switched to GED training, so that students in their final years of high school have the chance to access university education outside of Myanmar. Hence, students who were at university in Myanmar have returned to high school to get their GED as a means of restarting their higher education. Having to restart their university education and going back to school to qualify – an extremely frustrating experience – was also directly linked to students' inability to access university transcripts or any other official university documentation that might allow them to complete their degrees elsewhere. Most responding students said they had some sort of proof of what, where and how long they had studied in the form of emails, student cards or photos. However, since the coup it has been impossible for students who have left their studies to request official transcripts. An academic colleague based in Myanmar explained that universities had registered those students who had left and not taken the last set of exams as 'repeaters' – those who did not show up for the next set of exams would be expelled. In certain cases, students can get references from CDM staff or the NUG-affiliated university interim councils, as this quote from a former Myanmar academic explains:

> Personally, I give recommendations for students I know ... The university interim councils sometimes give recommendations or support. (INT MS)

Organisations working in the education field pointed to the lack of access to transcripts as a reason why students enrolled in schools or tried to get their GED to start their university education again in Thailand. However, those students who had studied for four or five years and were often just one exam away from graduation did not see this as an option. The need to get a degree to get on with life was seen as paramount, but the cost – both in money and time – to acquire it was often insurmountable.

Since attaining a GED and joining Thai universities is expensive, most students are unable to take this pathway. Responding students explained that they take online classes, some of which are offered by the Spring Universities (see Chapter 4), or other short courses – especially in languages (English, Thai, Japanese and Korean) or IT – with the hope to be able to continue their studies in a third country in the future. Students often discussed enrolling in online courses, some of which require certification of English, particularly if they are credit bearing. Respondents explained that online recorded lectures were a good option since they could revisit the content and adjust the learning to their work schedule.

> I would like to study online so I can choose my own schedule. I can also replay content I didn't understand. (FGD MS)

However, the online study mode also poses challenges, including isolation and mental health risks. Many find that fulfilling their core objective and honouring their identities as students are hampered by the factors discussed in the next section.

Modes of survival, challenges and risks

This section discusses some of the main challenges faced by the students as they navigate new lives far away from their homes and their universities. Leaving Myanmar was a hard decision for all of them, but since the risk of being arrested and spending many years in jail was high, students who had protested fled. After the shootings of peaceful protestors on the streets, described in the previous chapter, it had become clear that the SAC would use brutal means to punish those who did not accept the coup. It is hard to imagine the circumstances many have faced to arrive to the border. One female student explained how she had jumped from the first-floor window to evade the police at the front door:

> I jumped out of the first-floor window when they came to arrest me. I was not a leader, but they came. Now my family is at risk. (FGD MS)

Stories of students jumping from windows and balconies, sometimes to their deaths, were common shortly after the protests had been shut down by force (Associated Press 2021). With stories of torture in police stations and jails, fear of the authorities is real (Regan et al. 2021). These students are also incredibly concerned about the security of their families. Entering a non-SAC sanctioned programme can lead to repercussions from the SAC, even if the student is located outside the country. All respondents expressed fear for their families; they worried that their parents and siblings, or even distant relatives, would pay a high price when they, having fled, could not be arrested. Again, it was common to read of family members (including children) who were taken by the police or the military when the person the authorities were looking for could not be located.

Security (and digital security in particular) is therefore paramount; the fear of a security breach is real. During the fieldwork there was a security leak in one of the online school programmes running inside

Myanmar and responding students and organisations pointed to the repercussions this could lead to. The organisations who were interviewed explained that cameras always stay off for any online component, every participant has a code – names are never used – and only one administrator knows who the students are. The use of VPNs was also mentioned. Inside Myanmar this has become illegal, and whilst students do use VPNs to access certain social media sites, most programmes tried to make sure their content was available without the use of a VPN as this could lead to students being arrested.

Access to the internet and mobile phones has made it easier for students inside and outside Myanmar to stay in touch with their families back home, but this too carries risks; phones are often checked at checkpoints, and anyone caught communicating with the revolutionary students can face questioning and arrest. Travelling within Myanmar can also be dangerous. Even within certain cities students may have to pass through checkpoints, and meeting in groups is not allowed by the SAC. The security risks inside Thailand are not dissimilar for those who are undocumented. Having to hide from the Thai police and obtaining a police card by paying regular security fees is a requirement for anyone without a recognised ID. Meeting in groups poses extra security threats. The police card however does not protect them from arrest if they work without a permit. Organisations helping migrants and refugees on the border often have to step in and pay off the police after a student is arrested.

Few respondents spoke of the details of their transit to Thailand, only explaining how much they had paid brokers. The brokerage fee ranges between 2,000 and 10,000 Thai Baht per person. Once in Mae Sot, they tend to find accommodation, help and support amongst those who arrived before them. Most students live in shared accommodation with many to a room and no furniture – but together, they help each other survive. The main issue is money and how to earn it, both to pay for the bare necessities in life (such as rent and food) and to pay off the Thai police who might otherwise send them back, and also how to make enough money to send some to their families back home, who are affected by Myanmar's rampant inflation. This part of the story is similar across groups, from those who have left home to join the resistance to those who have stayed inside Myanmar, or even those who never left their families. The coup has made people poor and all must work to support themselves as well as their families. The economic situation inside Myanmar and on the border is dire – even the middle classes are struggling.

> What I am doing and what I want to do are totally different. I would like to study abroad, but because of money, political situations and different thing, I have to give up my dreams. I can't apply for jobs because I didn't graduate. I wish you all the best. We must win the Revolution. (Survey)

For the responding students, the type of work and the kind of remuneration differ depending on where they live. The amount required to cover rent, food, electricity, transport and internet varies depending on the context. At the time of writing, a general monthly figure for these basic needs inside Myanmar seems to be around $250–300 and in Thailand around 12,000 Thai Baht.[17] Students explained that they have had to accept work for lower wages because of their lack of registration and documentation, with Thai employers often taking advantage of their situation.[18] It is even more challenging for newly arrived students who do not speak Thai to find work, making them reliant on financial support from their families back in Myanmar, where the economic situation is bleak.

The lack of jobs also affects students inside the country. Young people have been lured to towns on the China border with promises of waitressing and hotel jobs only to find themselves hostages of gangs that force them into prostitution or online scamming work. The Chinese-speaking Myanmar youth were a particular target for recruitment as they were local and would have little recourse to law and order.[19] At the time of Operation 1027 (October 2023), the UN reported that as many as 120,000 people, many of them trafficked and held against their will, were involved in these scam centres on the Myanmar side of the border (OCHA 2023); the Kokang area on the Chinese border had become a particular hotspot.[20] It is their desperate need to earn money that drives young people to risk living away from their families in EAO-controlled zones. Whilst there have been some rescue operations in the meantime, it is unclear how many Myanmar youth remain hostages in such centres. The limelight of the most recent rescue operations on the Thai border has been on non-Myanmar nationals who had been illegally trafficked across the border.

To many it has become clear that if they want to earn money, get a decent job and find a future for themselves and their country, they need to either get a degree or manage somehow to finish a degree. Linked to the desire to continue studying (as described above) a new challenge has emerged – one they might not have encountered if they had remained at the Myanmar universities. Most respondents said they felt they had issues with their level of English. In Myanmar, university lectures are supposed to be delivered in English (British Academy and École Française d'Extrême-Orient 2015). In reality, this is not the case, as the level of English both of the students and the teaching academics is quite low (Lall 2021a). Responding students were forthright in explaining that communicating in English and studying in English were two completely different things. Those who had accessed Thai universities found it particularly challenging to have to engage with an unfamiliar university environment as well as to use English at that level.

> There are big differences between Myanmar universities and Thai universities. We all had a shock. (FGD CM)

There is also a barrier to getting the required English certifications or examinations, all of which cost money. Those who felt they had to start their degree from scratch and are preparing for the GED examination worry both about their English and the cost of it all. The special preparation required to pass the internationally recognised English exam is an additional challenge. Even some migrant education support services have started to help prepare students for these types of exams, as discussed in a later section. But Myanmar students are not used to these types of exams and their fear of failure is great. This is compounded by the learning loss sustained during the COVID pandemic, when all of Myanmar's universities were shut down and no one was able to attend any classes. Whilst the pandemic helped normalise online education, and this has resulted in many respondents taking some forms of classes they can access online, much of what they do has nothing to do with their original degree and is not relieving any of the learning loss they might have suffered.

Security issues pose a significant challenge for students living along the Thai border. Those with some form of Thai ID may feel relatively safer than those without, which is why students often strive to obtain some form of identification, as previously mentioned. However, even students in Mae Sot who possess ID cards can be arrested under various circumstances if they are unlucky. Among 37 students, 22 reported having experienced arrest: of these, nine held a 'police card', seven had a 'pink card', and one possessed both, but the police still came for them. Most of them were released after paying fines ranging from 500 to 12,000 Thai Baht. One student was deported but managed to return shortly thereafter.

Another challenge, mentioned first by the organisations that engage with the students and then some of the responding students themselves, is trauma and mental health. Both the students who have fled across the border, those inside on the border and those who have remained in their homes have lived through unimaginable trauma.

> Many students can't concentrate because of what they have experienced. (SU INT MS)

> Students have faced the atrocities, depression, students have the responsibility to look after their families. There is a lot of pressure. Both inside, outside, documented or not. Those who went to jail don't feel they can continue. (FGD MS)

Those who survived suffer from guilt. The guilt increases for those who are able to get on with their lives – for example, by enrolling in a Thai university.[21] Responding students did not speak about their mental health. In the FGDs they did, however, recount the horrors they have gone through.

> My brother was shot in the stomach in front of me. We were demonstrating peacefully. (FGD MS)

The trauma experienced by the students during the COVID pandemic – and more so during the coup, with friends and family dying or being arrested and their teachers joining the CDM – should not be underestimated. One of the Thai universities sheltering Myanmar students experienced the suicide of a Myanmar student they had supported; other organisations engaging with Myanmar students also report students feeling guilty, hopeless, depressed, suicidal and isolated. The poor, overcrowded conditions and the loneliness and homesickness take their toll. Whilst students support each other, they do not have access to professional help. Online course providers mentioned that droput levels were high, which could likewise lead to cycles of despair.

Towards the end of the time in the field, new challenges emerged. First, the SAC's new passport system. Myanmar passport offices were closed for a few months, causing severe anxiety amongst students already outside who needed to extend the validity of their documentation and who feared becoming stateless; it also caused concern amongst those inside looking for ways to leave. The passport offices have since reopened and new passports are being issued for particular purposes (business, study, religious etc.). However, they cannot be used for other reasons. The more general 'visit' passport, for example, might not be issued to students who want to leave, as the SAC is trying to retain control over who leaves and for how long. Responding students already explained that having a Myanmar ID card from a region that is currently in conflict with the Tatmadaw and the SAC would mean that a passport would not be issued, regardless of whether that student had been politically active or not.

Another challenge has been the implementation of the conscription law. As the Tatmadaw started to feel the strength of the resistance and began fighting battles across multiple fronts with many different groups, the need for more soldiers became apparent. The 2008 Constitution did have a clause mandating conscription of both boys and girls, but it was not activated until 2024. At the time of writing, all males aged between 18 and 35 and all females between 18 and 27 are targets for conscription. The term of conscribed service is said to be between two and three years but can be extended to five years during a state of emergency. Evading conscription is punishable by imprisonment and a fine. After the announcement of conscription coming into law in February 2024, the youth – and their parents – fell into a state of panic. Some tried to escape abroad (legally and illegally); others, especially ethnic minorities, decided to return to their hometowns from Yangon or other big cities to hide; and some decided to join PDFs since they would have to take up arms in any case (Linn 2024). And, ironically, some CDM students inside the country decided to return the SAC-run state universities to secure the temporary exemption from conscription provided to students.[22]

Additional challenges for students inside Myanmar

Many of the issues on the border apply inside Myanmar as well, but there are more and different issues – and arguably the risks for students who oppose the SAC are greater. The information detailed here was gathered through a survey run inside the country, but many responding students based on the Thai side of the border – and organisations run by students on the border – had friends inside and therefore could also give evidence as to the additional challenges for those inside Myanmar.[23] The following section details these additional challenges, many of which are interrelated.

In the first instance, there are issues directly related to the different levels of development between Thailand and Myanmar; the latter is poorer, and conflict-affected areas have had much of their infrastructure destroyed. Therefore, access to electricity and Wi-Fi varies widely across the country. Respondents described how many areas inside Myanmar only have a few hours of electricity per day. In areas that are not under SAC control, the Wi-Fi is usually cut. Access to Wi-Fi and electricity are better in Yangon, but students are not allowed to meet in groups.

> In Yangon joining online programmes will be less of a challenge, but other areas are more difficult. [*And coming to Yangon from outside?*] Landlords do not want to rent houses to young people. Youths are not allowed to meet in groups. (SU INT MS)

Given the urban warfare faced by revolutionary students, their chances of finding accommodation can be affected by the place they come from. In the preceding section on passports, the issue of coming from an area that is known to support the Revolution was mentioned. Getting an ID when living in or coming from the 'wrong area' can be impossible. Both in urban and rural Myanmar students are under close scrutiny whether they have been politically active or not. For those who did protest, evading police checks and detainment is a major part of daily life, as is fear of arrest and worse.

Outside of Yangon, there are air raids and bombardments in the areas to which the conflict has spread. This includes not only ethnic or border areas, but Magwe, Sagaing and other Bamar-majority areas that have been actively supporting the NUG. The country is at war. Students in these areas have to move regularly and may become homeless overnight.

In addition to the measures outlined, the SAC announced that private education institutions were no longer allowed to teach about Western democracy. Whilst the announcement concerns schools in the first instance, it is likely that any programme seen as promoting Western values or democracy could be seen as illegal, posing extra risk for students inside the country who are enrolled the social science online modules of non-Myanmar universities.

Migrant support services helping the revolutionary students

Thailand, and especially Mae Sot on the Thai–Myanmar border, has been receiving Myanmar nationals for decades. Whilst there have been waves of refugees, including a large number of students in the late 1980s and early 1990s, and regular influxes of mainly Karen villagers on the run from Tatmadaw attacks, the other main source of Myanmar migrants has been the workers coming to Thailand to earn money for their families back home. The refugees (or IDPs, as the Thai authorities prefer to call them) were originally housed in camps along the border. Migrants coming to work do not have access to the education and health support available inside the camps; consequently, numerous civil society-led organisations have sprung up along the border to assist these Myanmar nationals, regardless of their legal status.

These organisations, among which are the Mae Taw Clinic as well as many schools, have been overrun since the Myanmar coup.[24] Such schools are referred to as 'migrant learning centres' (MLCs), as this is the way they can register with the Thai authorities. The MLCs are administered by the Migrant Education Coordination Centre (MECC) that was set up 10 years ago within the Thai Ministry of Education. Respondents explained that there are 65 learning centres in Tak Province and that they had seen their intake more than double since the coup.[25] Tanaka (2023) describes how these MLCs have been essential in offering interim solutions for fleeing students. Some of these learning centres, or teachers working at them, have started to offer online classes (in certain cases also accessible inside Myanmar for students who are boycotting SAC schools) to broaden what is on offer. Teachers at some of the more established MLCs have also started to offer their own night classes online for students who have to work. Respondents mentioned that since COVID-19 had given them experience teaching remotely, they were better prepared to offer classes online. Of these 65, 3 were visited in person and are described here – Hsa Htoo Lei, New Blood School and the Children Development Centre (CDC).[26]

Founded in 1999, Hsa Htoo Lei is a learning centre for students from KG to Grade 12. At the time of writing, it had 1,090 students and around 55–60 teachers and admin staff. Student numbers had doubled after the coup. Originally this school served Myanmar migrants who had come to Thailand to work. Since the coup, it has also served Myanmar families who have fled. The MLCs use the Myanmar curriculum until Grade 8, adding other subjects such as Thai. The MLC used to prepare students for the Myanmar matriculation exam – students would return to take the exam at a school in Myawaddy, Myanmar, so that they could access Myanmar HEIs. With COVID, this became impossible, which is why Hsa Htoo Lei now prepares its secondary school students for the GED exam. Some of the students who have successfully taken the GED exam have managed to get into Thai universities. The school asks students to make a contribution of 1,000 Baht as a registration fee, 300 Baht per month for transportation as well as another 300 Baht for electricity and teacher salaries.

New Blood School is a migrant learning centre with 679 students. Between KG and Grade 7, it uses Myanmar's post-2015 NESP curriculum. Since the coup, it has offered GED training for the older students (of which were over 100 at the time of the fieldwork). Forty-eight students passed the GED. Newcomers may want to study for the GED but there are issues in paying for the examination fee and the transportation to the exam centre. Most of students are over 15 years old and are working as part-time waiters or performing other manual labour to survive, earning 150–200 Baht per day. The students who work can come to school only three days per week. These students face continual security concerns: such as the possibility of being arrested.[27] There are also students whose parents are on the Myanmar warrant list, their houses confiscated. Some have even experienced imprisonment. Most of the parents of New Blood School's students are on the run and all of them are jobless. As at Hsa Htoo Lei, prior to the coup, students at New Blood School would prepare for the Myanmar matriculation exam and take it once a year by crossing the border back into Myanmar; this has now become impossible. The school has 30 teachers who provide extra help to students for the GED classes. There are some student fees: 300 Baht per month for general schooling and 1,000 Baht per month for GED. There are more and more students but limited space; at the time of the research, 200 students lived in a compound supported by individual donors, who supply them with oil, rice and salt. Students grow vegetables for their kitchen, but they cannot produce enough for their needs. When we visited the school, more dormitories were under construction. Some of New Blood School's teachers who have fled Myanmar teach there in exchange for board and lodging.

The Children Development Centre (CDC) and the associated Mae Taw Clinic was started in 1995 as a learning centre running from KG to Grade 12. In the 2021–2 academic year it had 320 students; in 2022–3, enrolment rose to 997 students. This tripled intake is because of the coup. Grades 10 to 12 have seen a particular increase. Since not all of Thailand's 65 MLCs offer secondary schooling, CDC has seen a larger increase than others. GED training was started in September 2022 as a pilot programme and is now offered to students. 300 students have since passed the GED and there has been some financial support from the BEAM foundation. Some of those who register for the GED are students whose studies have been interrupted. CDC is the child protection and educational part of the Mae Taw Clinic, which USAID had funded via an NGO consortium. The clinic also receives funding from Canada, Germany and Japan; several embassies give small grants year by year. CDC raises funds abroad through Thai foundations and charities. A CDC staff member explained the challenges faced by the new arrivals, who differ markedly from the migrants that the school had been used to supporting:

> Without documents they [those who arrive] stay in safe house, but these are crowded. Some join the Thai government scheme for temporary employer. Some NGOs sponsor for documents. But that has stopped because they can't show this legally. Many organisations are under supervision of the Thai government. They get checked. They [those who arrive] use brokers to find employers. It's not easy. The risk is deportation. There are deportations every day. People are in hiding. Those who are prominent especially. Sometimes they are just returned. It depends on check points on the other side. If they are on the list, they can't come back ... Thai government are focused on the new arrivals, especially CDM, PDF, etc. they don't differentiate. Thai government is friendly with Myanmar government. They watch community-based organisations (CBOs) very closely. My clinic they tolerate, but we are being watched. (INT MS)

CDC also explained that it was different for organisations that were registered under a Thai foundation: 'Some centers like Minmahaw they are under a Thai foundation. That gives protection'. The headmaster of one of the schools agreed that security is the biggest risk for the newly arrived students and families:

> Security is the biggest problem. All students are illegal. They can arrest anyone over 15. Arrest and then [they need to pay a] bribe. We have problems every week with students who are arrested. We [the school] are a place where the police knows they can get money. When they [the students] go out – between apartment and school, as long as they go in uniform they are ok, but evening is not safe for them. (INT MS)

The schools described the needs of those crossing the border – again explaining that these needs were quite different from those of the original migrant population they had been supporting:

> They need shelter and food but they also need psycho-social support – there is guilt, and fear. Losing loved ones. They feel like they are not supposed to be here. They should be back there fighting. (INT MS)

The schools face new challenges. The large influx of Myanmar families with children, or teenagers on their own, has prompted schools to build dormitories to house them. A staff member from one school also spoke how fleeing teachers were staying and working at the school in exchange for food and lodging:

> Now there are more students, but limited space. Also other problems. Some students want good education, they cannot even afford to rent. Two-hundred students live in one compound [and are] supported by individual donors with oil and rice ... The school is growing vegetables for their kitchen. [But we face a] problem with getting land to grow. This year we cannot afford land rent, and there are more students to feed. (INT MS)

The participating MLCs have made some changes to their curricular offering. In particular, for the more senior high school classes, the GED curriculum has replaced the Myanmar government curriculum, since students can no longer return to Myanmar to take the matriculation exams and then continue on to Myanmar universities. GED training was also offered by a centre that offered two pathways for older schoolgoing children, but not the entire curriculum.

> It is impossible to re-join Myanmar university. If they want to join international university they need TOFL and GED. It is difficult to get proof they were students like transcripts; with GED they can start again. GED is the first step to start again and do what they want to do. (INT MS)

The GED qualification theoretically allows them to enrol at Thai universities, as long as they have the required IDs. This means that despite the costs involved in taking the exam, it is seen as the way forward for Myanmar students that are outside of the country. As mentioned previously, some students who had started university education inside Myanmar prior to the coup decided to go back to school and study for the GED, rather than hope for a pathway that would allow them to finish the degree they had started.

Aside from these learning centres (which operate like normal schools), there is also Minmahaw, an organisation established in 2007 to provide education for the children and grandchildren of Myanmar's political prisoners. As the political situation in Myanmar changed, Minmahaw started to support other children as well. They ran two programmes at the time of the fieldwork. One of these culminates in the internationally recognised high school GED exam. The second is a post-secondary programme that puts students on track for a career or university entrance but does not include training to take the GED exam. The programmes are aimed at the most underprivileged, those from camps, border towns, and more recently, those who have fled the country due to the coup, helping them access a university education. There were 29 students admitted to each programme, aged 17–23, out of over 200 applicants every year. The system uses a boarding school model and employs English immersion in its pedagogy. Minmahaw representatives explained that they try to maintain a gender balance and include different ethnic groups to break stereotypes. The students are taught autonomy, critical and creative thinking through experimental learning and extracurricular activities that require decision making and problem solving. Minmahaw also offers vocational studies, such as cooking classes.[28] Alumni join as staff and serve as role models. A staff member also explained the challenges faced by their students:

> Documentation is the largest problem. So many types of documents, new documents. Difficulty to reach with money, and lack of knowledge. Need someone to give you that documentation. Equivalency is also a problem. What does it mean Grade 10 in a migrant school, Myanmar and ethnic school? Students don't know what they have and how much value it has. (INT MS)

It is not only fleeing students who require support – teachers do too. For them, there is Teacher Focus, which offers migrant teacher assistance and training as well as supporting education research on the border. Teacher Focus also conducts work in the area of education quality assessment and youth empowerment. This includes capacity building for young people: training in ICT, leadership, teamwork and proposal writing, and mentorship for research skills. However, a respondent from the organisation noted that many of the young people they engage with have suffered from learning loss due to the gap of more than three years in their studies, commenting that 'they might have forgotten [a lot] and this is a challenge'. They acknowledge that accreditation is important:

> People had golden future. Before the coup there was agreement with ministry in Myanmar for migrants to go back. Most of schools here use NESP or old curriculum from Myanmar. (INT MS)

What this means is that before the coup, those abroad had a recognised path back to their country – back to getting jobs in Myanmar if they so chose or even to university if that was what they wanted. These bridges were broken by the coup, and alternative pathways had to be found. More on this will be presented in the next chapter.

Conclusion and analysis

This chapter has provided an overview of the realities faced by the Myanmar students, both those who stayed inside and those who fled abroad. The coup has destroyed whatever they had been working on, and many of them are at risk of arrest and worse.

For those who joined the armed resistance, their identity has irrevocably changed – they now are soldiers, and one can argue only the leaders of the PDF movements will use their heads to strategise to win the war. Soldiers are a key part of the resistance, but they have to follow orders. While there is a collective reimagining of a future Myanmar, and they are fighting for freedom and more equality, the framework used in this book only offers a limited understanding of their motives, identities and tactics as they form a part of Myanmar's youth movements as depicted by Novelli et al. (2024) – albeit with guns.[29]

It is different for those who did not take up arms, or those who, once injured and tired, put their gun down. The need to make a new life on the border without any money at their disposal has turned the student network into a lifeline. The theoretical framework helps us understand the lived experiences of these refugee students – how they make meaning of their new post-coup situation. It also helps explain how education defines their identity and why education is at the heart of their resistance.

Beyond the student experience, the framework clarifies how the migrant institutions that try to help the students have had to pivot away from the Myanmar curriculum and offer alternative pedagogies. Whilst the schools now focus on preparing the youth for the GED, to try to open up ways into universities outside of Myanmar, the NGO-led programmes offer the kind of critical thinking and youth empowerment programmes that can equip their students with the kind of intellectual skills that are required to survive in their precarious new situation. The alternative pedagogies offered by Minmahaw and Teacher Focus are just selected examples from a much wider offering. However, all the migrant programmes on offer are limited by the fact that they are run by people who have not experienced the Revolution and the street protests personally. They support those affected, many of whom are part of the active youth protest movement, but the actual meaning and knowledge making of the Revolution happens elsewhere. The next chapter turns to alternative higher education provision, in particular the Spring Universities and their role in supporting and maintaining the Revolution.

Notes

1 The refugee camps are not officially accepting any newcomers. However, some respondents who engage with the camps informed us that the population number in the camps did increase after the coup, suggesting that some displaced people stay in a camp if they have some personal networks with camp residents. This information and the information on the third country settlement scheme was obtained in August 2022, when one of the authors visited Mae Sot.

2 A similar type of ID card was issued in Ranong in southern Thailand for a certain period, but it had no legal effect in Thailand (Fujita et al. 2010). These cards are issued solely at the discretion of local authorities. We did not find a similar card in Chiang Mai or Chiang Rai.

3 The Non-Thai ID card (pink) and the work permit (white) are different documents, but there appears to be some confusion or inconsistencies in their use. Under the proper process, workers without a valid passport must first obtain a Certificate of Identity from the Myanmar Embassy. They then submit this, along with their smart card (a biometric data card required for border crossing introduced since 2024), to the Thai Department of Employment to obtain a work permit, which is valid for two years. Only after securing the work permit can they apply for the Non-Thai ID card. The Non-Thai ID card is valid for 10 years but does not grant the right to work without a valid work permit. For students in exile who have fled their country, obtaining a Certificate of Identity from the Myanmar Embassy is not an option. This suggests the existence of loopholes in the process, potentially creating a demand for brokers.

4 This literally means a 'village card' issued by the head of the village. It was originally intended for seasonal agricultural labourers who cross the border during the peak farming season.

5 For experiences inside Myanmar see Chambers and Saw Ner Dhu Da (2024). The article focuses on how young people in Karen State navigate revolutionary life, how they initiated protests and joined CDM, organised themselves digitally, and faced the harsh realities of armed conflict.

6 A colleague inside Myanmar was asked to collect informal data from students and their families who have re-joined SAC universities.

7 Interviews in Mizoram, India in November 2024.

8 Htet Lynn Oo (2023) proposes a 'triangle model' for Myanmar's post-coup struggle, integrating armed struggle, non-violent civil disobedience, and diaspora-led transnational advocacy, arguing that these three strands operate collaboratively, reinforcing each other. This is, of course, true in part; however, there are also deep divisions between and within the resistance forces as described by Thawnghmung and Robinson (2025) in their work on the fragmented post-coup landscape.

9 The International Crisis Group (2021a, 2021b) documented the rapid rise of armed militias in response to the military's brutal suppression of peaceful protests post-coup, focusing on new resistance dynamics, including the formation of village-based defence forces and their guerrilla tactics, often supported by local knowledge and resources. Subsequent ICG reports, such as ICG (2024a) show the territorial gain and the role played by the EAOs that have in part fought along side the PDFs.

10 Connelly and Loong (2023, ch. 6) provide a comprehensive overview of Myanmar's post-coup conflict, mapping the roles of various EAOs, the PDFs and the NUG. They identify three conflict zones: borderland strongholds, contested central regions and non-aligned areas. They estimate that there are at least 95,000 PDF troops in total, consisting of approximately 65,000 PDF fighters allied with the NUG, 30,000 LDF fighters operating independently and an unknown number of PDT members.

11 For example, the KPDF is under the command of the Kachin Independence Army (KIA), the CDF is under the control of Chinland Joint Defence Committee (CJDC) and the KNDF is closely affiliated with the Karenni Army (KA) of the Karenni National Progressive Party (KNPP).

12 This reflects the chasm of the late 1980s and early 1990s, when Daw Aung San Suu Kyi called for democracy first, and the resolution of ethnic grievances later, once the democratic government had been established. For the EAOs and the ethnic groups they fight for, the priority is the restitution of their ethnic rights, autonomy and the recognition of the decades of injustice they have had to endure.

13 Chin has been divided into two camps over the course of the Revolution: the Chinland Council (with its armed wing, the CNF/CDF) and the Interim Chin National Consultative Council (with its armed wing, the Chin Brotherhood). This division has occasionally led to clashes (Lovett 2025). However, in February 2025, the two groups reached an agreement to establish a unified body called the 'Chin National Council'. While this marks a significant step toward unity, the effectiveness of the agreement remains to be seen and requires ongoing monitoring (Myanmar Now 2025).

14 See also the ICG (2024a) report, which emphasises the fact that the growing autonomy of ethnic groups does not automatically lead to inter-ethnic violence but rather reflects a continuation of Myanmar's long-standing state fragmentation. The armed resistance by ethnic groups, often coordinated through alliances like the Three Brotherhood Alliance, has been decisive in breaking the military's hold on borderlands. However, this decentralisation complicates prospects for a unified federal state, suggesting that any future political settlement must reckon with entrenched ethnic autonomy and the reality of subnational governance.

15 According to an interview conducted in November 2025 in Mizoram, a village in Chin State with a population of about 1,000, most residents were evacuated to another location in December 2021 due to armed conflicts. The villagers formed their own PDF, which has been incorporated into a larger group. Currently, around 30 people are members of the PDF, and the villagers collectively support the costs of uniforms, food, and medical care for the injured. So far, three members have been killed and eight have been injured.

16 The GED (General Educational Development) test consists of four subject-based tests that, once passed, give a high school equivalency credential. The four subjects are language arts, math, social studies and science.

17 It was emphasised that the stipend for inside Myanmar needs to be calculated in dollars or euros because of the instability of the MMK.

18 On the challenges of Myanmar migrant workers as a whole, please refer to UNDP (2023).

19 Since 2023 the network of scam centres has expanded vastly, with young people from all over the world being tricked into coming to Bangkok and then trafficked across the border to Myanmar's Shwe Koko zone and held there as hostages. The Economist's podcast *Scam Inc.* has detailed how the scamming now targets Western countries as much as China, with English speaking skills required.

20 The ICG claims that China allowed the EAO operation to take place in order to get better control over the criminal groups running these scam centres (International Crisis Group 2024b).

21 One Thai programme experienced a suicide.

22 Clause 15(a) of People's Military Service Law (State Peace and Development Council Law No. 27/2010), http://www.asianlii.org/mm/legis/laws/pmslpadcln272010638/. It was amended in January 2025.

23 There were 70 respondents: Age range 16–27; 40 Bamar, 14 other ethnic identifications; 56 Buddhists, 4 Muslims, 5 Christians; 24 male, 45 female, 1 other. Range of parental background from manual labour to middle class. Students from 22 different universities and 23 different subjects of study. A few high school graduates also responded.

24 They cannot register as schools because they do not teach in Thai or the Thai curriculum. They are referred to as MLCs by the authorities, but because they really are schools, we are using the term 'school' in this volume.

25 The initial effort to set up schools was made by the Burmese Migrant Workers' Education Committee (BMWEC), which serves as umbrella organisations for 30 MLCs, serving over 6,000 students as of 2024–5. On the history of MBWEC, see https://www.bmwec.org/bmwec_history/.

26 Since the fieldwork was conducted there have been changes to the MLCs described here. Some of them are now administered under Thai foundations and it seems that there has been

increased funding to meet the needs of those accessing the MLCs. Research by an UCL IOE MA student in the summer of 2025 showed that most classrooms now had better technological equipment and that there was less overcrowding than in 2023. Some of the issues described here, however, persist, in particular with regard to teacher salaries, with CDM teachers still teaching for board, lodging and pocket money.

27 The schools explained that they have someone being arrested every week.

28 This is jointly done with Hospitality and Catering Training Centre, which has been providing hospitality training to Karen youth since 2008.

29 In Wells (2021), education is discussed as both a battleground for competing political narratives as well as a means of shaping future citizens. Wells details how student activism in the Spring Revolution is framed within these competing political narratives, with students often siding with the equality narrative, demanding systemic change beyond procedural democracy. As seen from the quotes, this is also reflected in the voices collected for this book.

4

Reclaiming higher education: student-led provision and other solutions to support the Revolution

> 'I would say the Spring Revolution, it brought so much horror but it also places a new hope for us, because it brought many new things for us that people were not prone to before, like the spring universities.'

Key actors of the Spring Revolution are the students and Gen Z activists who grew up during the decade of reform, an unprecedented moment of transformations, including the betterment of educational opportunities, political liberalisation, the expansion of spaces for critical thinking and freedom of speech and rapid digital development (Lall 2021a), some of which were detailed in Chapter 1. The changes to Myanmar as a country and to Myanmar society were both profound and incomplete; political participation was encouraged, but democracy was not on offer. Students who grew up in the decade preceding the reforms experienced freedom of speech and a lack of fear of the government, as well as different forms of globalisation – the country opened up to the world and some urban centres began to look like the other cities in Southeast Asia. Many became aware that the building of a new Myanmar was a work in progress, but the direction of travel had been set and the aim was to make Myanmar a country that could hold its own in ASEAN and the rest of the world.

As discussed in Chapter 2, after the coup, young people started to boycott the junta-controlled educational system. Their behaviour in response to the brutal military takeover went beyond the strikes and protests documented in the media; rather, they showed how the seeds planted during the reform period had sprouted. One of these 'sprouts' was the realisation of the value and power of education.

When they realised that the 'Revolution is taking longer than expected' (INT MS), groups of exiled students started to create new higher education opportunities for CDM students both inside and outside Myanmar. The COVID experience had made the whole world more adept at using digital resources in education and communication; this was also the case in Myanmar. Since education could be delivered online, students who did (do) not want to return to SAC universities, or those who were (are still) displaced or have left the country would be able to continue their higher education journeys. The situation is exemplified by the quotation presented at the beginning of this chapter, voiced by a student interviewed by a student in Yangon (Proserpio 2025, p. 116).

The organisations that have been branded 'Spring Universities' (taking their name from the 'Spring Revolution') are online educational institutions created after the coup by CDM students, CDM university professors, and educational practitioners, sometimes with the help of international faculty. A recent report on higher education published by Spring University Myanmar (2023) maps what they call 'Interim Education Providers' (IEP) as alternatives to the institutions controlled by the SAC. They include Ethnic Education departments, online education platforms, interim university councils and student unions, ministries under the National Unity Government (NUG), and community initiatives in conflict areas. Whilst all these IEPs are engaged in a groundbreaking educational re-imagining (Wong and Kareng 2023), this chapter focuses first on the HEI online platforms created by the students for their peers. It discusses the activities of the Spring Universities, focusing on three specific case studies: the Burma Academy, the Spring University Myanmar (SUM) and the Irrawaddy Law School (ILS). All three were founded and are run by students – an unprecedented development not only in Myanmar history, but also in the recent history of other student protests and resistance movements.[1] The chapter also engages with the Minority Affairs Institute (MAI), founded by a CDM professor from the University of Yangon, before describing some of the work done by the NUG's Spring Normal University, which is trying to recreate teacher training for Myanmar schools in NUG-controlled areas.

In mapping these new institutions, the chapter discusses the educational re-imagining that these institutions are creating and the principles they are based on. At their core, all of them include teaching content with a focus on discourses on inclusion and social justice. Their educational programmes acknowledge the importance of preparing students to solve the problems of contemporary Myanmar, and students are introduced to concepts such as federalism and just peace.

The teaching and learning experience are supported and enhanced by the savvy use of IT tools and social media.

Finally, the chapter discusses how these new visions for higher education – visions that are deeply rooted in the idea of an education suited to a federal and just society – are even more transformative than the ones at the basis of the country's recent higher education reforms, as described in Chapter 1.

The Spring Universities: a new way to provide higher education

Student-organised or student-led higher education primarily targets those inside Myanmar, who are deemed to be even less fortunate than those who made it out. These new learning platforms vary in the specific subjects that they concentrate on: Irrawaddy Law School, as the name implies, focuses on delivering courses on law, while others are broader and offer courses that help students maintain their learning in the areas they had studied before. Many also offer short courses (Spring University Myanmar) or vocational courses (Burma Academy) that can be completed online in addition to a wider curriculum. Some of these institutions have been experimenting with novel technology to make their programmes accessible to areas in Myanmar without internet. All student-led platforms are exploring pathways to the accreditation of their courses and modules, showing how important the formal recognition of their degree is to students.

Spring University Myanmar (SUM) (not to be confused with Spring Normal University, discussed further subsequently) was co-founded in May 2021 by a group of Myanmar students who had fled to Thailand, some quite early on after the coup. They started by offering online certificate courses with a range of teaching faculty from Myanmar

Table 4.1 Growth of Burma Academy (BA), Irrawaddy Law School (ILS) and Spring University Myanmar (SUM) as of September 2024. Reproduced from Marie Lall, Aung Mann, M., and Proserpio, L. (2025, p. 9). 'Emerging from adversity: Spring Universities in post-coup Myanmar', *Education and Conflict Review*, 5, p. 91

	Students in 2022	Students in 2024	Faculty in 2022	Faculty in 2024	Courses in 2022	Courses in 2024
BA	15,000	45,000	15	60	30	90
ILS	274	94	9	8	11	4
SUM	8,956	3,292	184	143	267	108

universities across 12 disciplines, with courses lasting 5–10 weeks. They have also developed a nine-month diploma programme covering HR, local government, community development and federalism. It is clear that these subjects have been chosen with a view to what Myanmar will need for future rebuilding. Anyone who wants to take the courses on offer is welcome (although there are fees for those who can pay). The founders confirmed: '*Students don't need an undergraduate degree to join, it depends on their competency*' (SU FGD CM).

> SUM was founded with the mission of providing alternative education to Myanmar youths and for the past three years, our priority has been to promote 'access' to these alternative education resources for all student groups, including those from urban areas, ethnic regions, religious minorities, displaced populations (both internal and cross-border), and youth leaders active in the Spring Revolution. (SU FGD CM)

SUM has arranged a university partnership with Chiang Mai University and at the time of writing was co-delivering credit-bearing programmes with Arizona University that can subsequently be used towards a degree. One of the latest additions to the curriculum was a course on Public Health Management in Crisis, again reflecting the priorities of the coup. The target audience are CDM doctors working in the conflict zones. The course is offered in Burmese so as to benefit a wide audience. They also work with technology that can enable digital learning where the internet is not available – adopting, for example, the Raspberry Pi system, which offers its own Wi-Fi hotspot and can give access to online classroom in areas without internet. They also offer radio lectures through local shortwave radio. In the 'liberated areas' of Karenni State and Sagaing Region they have started to pilot face-to-face courses. Their funds come from student fees, but these are waived for students who can't pay. They are also supported financially by the Hanns Seidel Foundation (Germany), IDEA (Sweden) and IDRC (Canada).[2]

Burma Academy is a second student-led HEI, offering a wide array of courses for learners from all walks of life. Their courses are modelled after the massive open online courses (MOOCs) that have recently been changing access to global education. In fact, their main goal is to become Myanmar's leading MOOC platform, providing free education to diverse learners. Much of their teaching models is asynchronous and only available in Burmese, a different approach to that which predominates at SUM. This means they can offer their courses to a larger number of students, including those who might not be able to connect to a virtual classroom at a particular time and those who do not speak English. What they offer is also completely free of charge. As the founders explained:

> The Burma Academy is an online learning platform for a wider audience. Zoom classes are limited because of internet and electricity. We are providing education for a mass audience all in Burmese. It is for students inside the country who are hindered because of COVID and coup. We focus on two areas. Political based courses. Promoting federalism, human rights, ethnic studies ... We also offer vocational courses like programming, photoshop, video editing, accounting, languages – Thai, Japanese Korean ... Everything is recorded and alternative ways like zoom hybrid learning methods are available. We have weekly discussion sessions but it is self-paced. Recordings are accessible to all. There are 20,000 students registered on the website. (SU FGD MS)

Burma Academy offers different types of courses – those developed entirely by the Burma Academy with support from CDM academics; collaborative courses that are developed with academic partners; and complete partner courses provided by local academic partners hosted on the Burma Academy platform. Additionally, there are adapted courses (based on the curricula of accredited international academic institutions) and translated international courses (hosted on Burma Academy's platform), both of which have official approval. Burma Academy's translation team provides the Burmese subtitles.

At the time of writing, Burma Academy's number of registered students has grown to more than 40,000. Students come from both inside and outside Myanmar and are enrolled in 129 courses. Burma Academy's model of accessible, systematic and effective learning experiences clearly caters to a wide Myanmar audience. More recently, a few courses have been offered synchronously via community centres inside Myanmar in areas not under SAC control, but most courses remain based on self-paced online learning. A 'BA box' is also in development, using the Raspberry Pi technology that enables students' access to online content without an internet connection (similar to what SUM has been using).

Burma Academy has also been working on creating strategic alliances and partnerships with international organisations and universities to ensure that their programmes reflect excellence, in contrast to

Myanmar higher education of the past, which was largely insular and devoid of such standards. To achieve the aforementioned aims, Burma Academy representatives explain that they are working to establish a resilient organisational infrastructure that allows 'the growth of the talents and organization towards enduring success' ('Burma Academy presentation' 2024).

The ILS focuses on Constitutional Law for understanding federalism, International Human Rights Law, and other international laws for raising rights-based awareness and promoting gender equality for community building. Their courses also explore various aspects of international law, including peacekeeping and transitional justice.

> We set up in 2021 by contacting teachers who were part of CDM. This [what they offer] is for CDM student interim learning in law, Human Rights, international law, introduction to political knowledge as well as research methods. Per course there are around 14–25 students. Two-hundred-and-forty students are registered, most are inside [Myanmar]. Only a few are outside. (SU FGD MS)

In the case of all three HEIs depicted here, learning how to run a university has been a new experience for their student leaders. None of the founders had any kind of management experience; they had mostly been active in the students' unions of their universities, where they had advocated for students' rights (Lall et al. 2025). Setting up a university came with big responsibilities and a steep learning curve. But as respondents explained, they saw no alternative if they wanted to start shaping the future of Myanmar. The creation of these student-led HEIs was driven by three key factors: guilt and responsibility; the will to build a system based on inclusion and social justice for a federal Myanmar of the future; and the potential to offer a better learning and teaching experience by using modern technologies. Each one of these will now be discussed in turn.

Guilt and responsibility

Guilt and responsibility have been major drivers in the setting up and development of these student-led HEIs. Respondents described their feelings of responsibility for the peers they had left behind in Myanmar, above all for those in hiding or on the run.[3] While some did not use the word 'guilt', others did – and it quickly became clear that there was a complex set of emotions that drove them to think beyond their own personal ambitions and futures.

> Our challenges are – mental well-being. Student lives here [on the border] are precarious. The situation is difficult. We will get survival when our peers can't. Then there is academic workload, living different lives when others are being tortured. Suicide risk. Guilt. (SU FGD CM)

> Students have faced the atrocities, depression, students have the responsibility to look after their families. There is a lot of pressure. Both inside, outside, documented or not. Those who went to jail don't feel they can continue. (SU FGD MS)

The feelings were particularly intense for those who had survived shootings in the street or evaded arrest. The guilt mixed with feelings of responsibility increased for those who had been able to get on with their lives; for example, by enrolling in a university or finding some other form of safety after crossing the border. This galvanised some students to come together and create alternative HEIs. The message from all is a sense of responsibility for the future of their country and a desire to contribute to meaningful change through education. In certain cases, their sense of responsibility goes beyond education:

> Since the Revolution is taking longer, we also provide vocational and practical training for career pathways. Also another category – to contribute to the Revolution, well-being in IDP camps, we provide water purification for youths in ethnic areas or camps. (SU FGD MS)

Foundations of inclusion and social justice for the future of a federal Myanmar through education

All respondents involved in these student-led HEIs see their work as part of the building up of a better and more inclusive future Myanmar; debates on federalism and what kind of country Myanmar should become are at the heart of what they offer. The curricula across the three institutions are designed to foster inclusion and social justice, while encouraging debate on critical issues such as federalism and minority rights. Their founders explained that the principles of inclusion and social justice are embedded into their teaching methods as well.[4]

Representatives of Spring University Myanmar state that they promote inclusivity through flexible admissions policies, allowing CDM students without formal qualifications to enrol. During the FGD SUM confirmed their vision: '*Regardless of the platform – SAC, NUG, or online – young people must have access to lifelong learning*.' This inclusive approach helps students to continue studying despite the political disruption. SUM offers diploma courses in human rights, peace studies and federalism, reflecting the needs of a future Myanmar. The development of action-based research practices is supported by combining theoretical learning with community-based research and community-based initiatives, and students are encouraged to apply their knowledge to practical efforts aimed at rebuilding the country. This ensures that education remains practical and relevant as well as serving the wider Myanmar community.

Burma Academy's focus on social justice is reflected in its no-fee policy. Courses are designed with marginalised groups in mind, including in remote and conflict-affected areas. At the heart is the Revolution – they term what they offer 'ideological courses, which focus on promoting federal democratic principles, human rights, and equality.[5] This includes discussions of what had happened to the Rohingyas, one of the thorniest subjects in debates on Myanmar ethnic and religious relations and citizenship. The idea is to foster a societal shift towards inclusive values and support for diverse groups through education, by breaking the traditionally held Myanmar beliefs about ethnic hierarchies and the role of the military in society. Practical skills in service to the Revolution are provided through essential training for combat medics and education in digital security, mental health and health education. These are designed to support individuals in conflict zones and equip them with vital skills.

The ILS's curriculum equips students to use the law to advocate for social justice. By admitting students from conflict-affected areas, the ILS promotes inclusion while addressing legal frameworks essential to protecting vulnerable populations. Their courses actively engage students in debates around constitutional law, humanitarian law and transitional justice. These discussions are crucial for understanding the legal frameworks necessary to rebuild a democratic and federal Myanmar. The ILS founders have also started an affiliated research institute that will feed into the teaching. This institute is not yet independently funded but shows that ILS understands the importance of research in delivering high-quality educational content.

Using IT to offer a better teaching and learning experience

Poor learning and teaching experiences had been the norm at Myanmar universities, even after the reforms. Improving this aspect of education has therefore been a priority for new institutions, which have fostered research and developed practical vocational programmes to build a better future for Myanmar. More importantly, much of the resulting pedagogical improvement has been brought about by leveraging technology. The COVID pandemic taught students and academics around the world how to deliver internet-based education, both through live platforms such as Zoom and courses designed for those who might not be able to attend classes during fixed times. This 'pandemic training' has been instrumental in allowing the student-led HEIs to develop their own models, and by learning from the platforms of other international universities, to strive for a quality higher than previous Myanmar universities had offered.

The use of IT by these institutions enables students to continue learning despite significant challenges like internet restrictions, political instability and security threats. Gen Z is generally more IT-savvy than preceding generations, and learning can happen on a mobile phone, a laptop, a tablet in a student's home or elsewhere, without the need for physical buildings or a library. With that said, Myanmar universities had never offered great infrastructure in the first place, with most libraries bare of books, deficient in internet access and lacking in IT services, even after the reforms. This meant that the students thrown out of their universities by the coup would not miss out on much in the way of basic technological resources.

As large online learning platforms, SUM and Burma Academy offer hundreds of courses to thousands of students inside Myanmar, many of whom have no other access to higher education under the SAC regime. More advanced technology has also allowed SUM to develop digital learning tools that provide offline access to courses in low-connectivity areas. This technological innovation ensures that students in the most remote regions can continue their studies, providing an alternative to traditional internet-based education.

Furthermore, the use of IT has allowed these HEIs to experiment with different types of courses, focused on delivering a good education experience with student needs in mind. The education on offer no longer resembles the passive, lecture-based learning traditionally provided by Myanmar universities. CDM teachers involved in these universities have had to engage with new forms of teaching and learning. The founders of Burma Academy talked about the capacity building required for CDM teachers, which went beyond anything they would have experienced in the traditional pre-coup Myanmar system. The founders of ILS described how they had started to provide higher education using Zoom and Google for recorded files, as all their teaching is online.

> Currently, we are using Zoom for live classroom sessions. For classroom communication, assessments, and sharing learning materials, we are utilising Google Classroom. However, we are exploring ways to advance our school's technology. According to our plans, we aim to develop an educational information system and e-campus to enhance efficiency for both lecturers and students. Unfortunately, due to financial constraints, we are unable to move into advanced learning technology. As a result, we are currently relying on traditional online learning methods, using free-version tools to navigate toward our institutional education goals. (SU FGD MS)

All student-led HEIs have had to learn how to engage students in critical thinking and analytical skills through classroom discussions and group work – even if the classes are asynchronous. Some have started to include research and research training as a part of their courses, new to most students since traditional Myanmar universities did not offer much on that score.

Challenges

All three organisations face similar challenges. At the top of the list is the security risk for all those involved, whether inside or outside Myanmar. Since these platforms are illegal inside Myanmar, both the volunteers working on the platforms in any capacity and any student accessing the platforms risk arrest. This is compounded by the fact that VPNs are illegal in Myanmar but are required to access the blocked websites hosting educational content. The interaction between the mainly anonymous (for security reasons) volunteers inside the country and those working at the head offices in Thailand was a particular difficulty for Burma Academy in terms of their delivery model, as it resulted in communication and coordination issues. Managing the IT system in a safe way has been imperative. Respondents explained that one online school had their security breached, with names of enrolled students falling into the hands of the SAC. This was followed by a wave of arrests. The SAC is actively going after education platforms, including via cyber-attacks. All student-led HEIs have had their websites and Facebook pages targeted.

The students who set up the higher education platforms under discussion are based in Thailand, where they should be safe. But arrest is not only a risk for those inside Myanmar. Since these students are not recognised as refugees in Thailand, they have had to find ways to get some sort of recognised residential status. Upon arrival, none of the students had long term visas and risked arrest for living in Mae Sot or Chiang Mai illegally. As described in Chapter 3, they usually paid to acquire 'police cards' or other ID in Mae Sot. Nevertheless, all of them had been arrested at some point – they had to be bailed out by their friends so as not to be deported to Myanmar. Whilst this situation has improved, with a number of individual residential statuses changed, most of those working for the student-led HEIs are still stateless or in precarious visa situations. As anti-SAC activists, the risks they face are even greater than those of other students.

Whilst these are the main existential risks, there are many other issues, such as organisational registration, which is impossible inside Myanmar and difficult in Thailand. As the founders of BA explained, this is required for both legal compliance and official recognition. Without such registration, academic accreditation of the courses they offer remains impossible. Yet students continuing their studies on these platforms do need some sort of internationally recognised credits for their studies to 'count' and be used towards a degree. The lack of an internationally recognised higher education accreditation system makes it impossible for even the Tokyo-based United Nations University to help[6]. SUM has managed to get some sort of credit system organised for some courses through its partnership with Arizona University, but this does not apply to courses offered in Burmese by Myanmar CDM academics – yet courses in Burmese are what are most needed for a student body that cannot understand enough English to really learn and understand academic content. International collaboration and partnerships are therefore important but do not necessarily resolve the key issue of official accreditation.

Finally, financing the endeavour is a key challenge. All student-led HEIs are applying for grants to pay for hardware, internet, office space and electricity. This takes a lot of time and effort and there are no guarantees of success. Moreover, the amounts of money secured are often small. Such grants do not help with salaries and all student-led

HEIs are completely dependent upon an unpaid volunteer workforce – which, given the size of the platforms and their rate of growth, is not sustainable. Representatives of Burma Academy added that there has been higher turnaround of the workforce in recent times, due to the repetitive nature of the work and competing priorities. In order to keep trained volunteers on board and to become a properly professional organisation, salaries need to be paid.

Tertiary learning platforms run by former Myanmar university staff

Former Myanmar academics have also created educational platforms. Three former Myanmar university professors based on the Thai–Myanmar border explained how they had set up (separate) online learning platforms for Myanmar students both inside and outside to continue their studies. Their platforms had different aims – one was particularly focused on supporting minorities but also emphasised teaching ordinary Myanmar students about Myanmar's multi-ethnic, multi-cultural and multi-religious society. Courses cover topics like federalism, ethnic minority politics in Myanmar and human rights, including freedom of religion and belief.

> I want to fill the minority issue requirement. Give political awareness. Not only majority but also minority need their space. Including education and critical thinking. Right political thinking to create harmony. (INT MS)

The aim of the institute is to highlight the struggles of Myanmar's ethnic minorities. By including Rohingya students, it fosters an inclusive educational environment that amplifies marginalised voices. This has become particularly important; even the inclusive discourse of those fighting for the Revolution (including the NUG) still does not include minorities who do not fit the traditional ethnonational model based on 'homelands', despite the sacrifices they have made in resisting the SAC (Aung Ko Ko et al. 2024). The founder of the Minority Affairs Institute (MAI) believes that the political solution for Myanmar lies in federalism. Hence, the courses on offer explain this concept and focus on community building and the representation of minorities in politics, so that students can engage in debates on peaceful coexistence with a better understanding of these ideas. One tool used by MAI in its basic research skills training course asks students to analyse federalism from the minority perspective. The founder of MAI believes that trying to see the country through the eyes of minorities will lead to greater political acceptance of Myanmar's diverse population.

Other interim solutions

The student-led HEIs and platforms discussed previously are part of the Revolution's interim higher education space. However, the NUG's ministry of education has also set up shadow institutions to try to help students finish their degree and get the credits corresponding to the work they have done.[7] A female respondent in one FGD observed that '*the NUG try as much as they can to make education accessible*' (FGD MS). One interim solution adopted by CDM academics has been to set up Interim University Councils (Nora 2023). These bodies help their former students by certifying what they had been taught – a useful feature when students can no longer ask for transcripts from their institutions, now under SAC control.[8] Delinking education from the military regime is part of the wider NUG's education strategy and policy, which defines their vision of 'a well-educated, peaceful, democratic, and prosperous Myanmar society where all individuals can contribute to civic and economic life' and mission to 'build a regionally and globally competitive workforce and an educated citizenry through a diverse and democratic federal education system'.[9]

According to their website, the NUG's education policy core goals and objectives are to build a federal education system that is democratic, inclusive and equitable; support the participants of the CDM, especially educators, by providing safe zones, salaries and recognition; ensure access to education for children and youth through online, virtual and in-person alternatives in liberated or contested areas; develop policy frameworks and governance structures that reflect the federal democratic values outlined in the Federal Democracy Charter (2021); support inclusive and multilingual education, with a strong emphasis on ethnic languages and cultural autonomy; and advance human resources and institutional development for a resilient and decentralised education sector.

These principles reflect values that did not previously exist within Myanmar's education system, even after the reforms. For example, the policy quoted previously explicitly acknowledges the longstanding lack of equal opportunities that has existed prior and the existence of discrimination based on ethnicity and religion. As discussed in Chapter 1, the failure of the Thein Sein reforms was due in part to the absence of decentralisation and inadequate recognition of local realities such as language. The NUG policy has taken this on board, as well as the principle of institutional autonomy for HEIs.

Closer collaboration with non-state organisations such as CSOs and ethnic education providers has resulted in the NUG Ministry of Education establishing nearly 6,000 interim community-based schools across liberated and resistance-controlled areas, serving over 750,000 students with the support of more than 60,000 teaching staff. It has likewise developed online and virtual school programmes, ensuring continued access to education for students nationwide. With regard to higher education, the NUG has launched 201 interim educational facilities offering university-level education, with over 100,000 students enrolled. Collaborations with entities like the Karenni State Interim Executive Council and the Ta'ang Education Academy have been pivotal in these efforts (Burma News International 2024). Nyan Lynn Thit Analytica (2022a), however, notes that the efforts to build alternative schooling systems in liberated areas are often uneven and underfunded, indicating the difficulties the NUG is facing with on-the-ground education delivery. Spring Normal University (SNU), the first HEI created by the NUG, opened in September 2021. Also known as Myanmar Nway-Oo University, it was set up by the NUG with help from the staff of the Yangon and Sagaing Universities.[10] Its vice chancellor is Dr Thein Lwin, a long-time critic of the Myanmar education system (Lall 2021a). SNU focuses on teacher training by collaborating with the CDM staff from the 25 Education Degree Colleges (EDCs) across the country.[11] Their main aim is to provide and support teacher training so that schools in NUG-controlled areas have competent teachers capable of using methodologies different from those employed in SAC-held zones. In a meeting, they explained that the programme is future focused, as teachers who are supportive of the Revolution's mission will be essential in changing Myanmar's basic education system from the ground up. SNU has developed a basic programme that focuses on 'the nine competencies of a good teacher', which is delivered through an NUG Ministry of Education webinar and a handbook, allowing teachers to learn at their own pace. They also provide support to CDM teachers who need capacity building in liberated areas. The training is offered in both synchronous and asynchronous format over Zoom. On the border with Thailand, they have developed a training of teachers backpack programme to support teachers who could not otherwise access training. The NUG has also recognised and given support to the Spring Universities, both as a way for students to avoid SAC HEIs and as a legitimate part of the broader Spring Revolution movement. These collaborations paint a picture that differs radically from Myanmar's traditional education policy, including the post-2012 reformed reality across the education sector. Federalism and inclusion seem to be at the core of the NUG's approach, and there is an understanding that education is both a tool of empowerment and of resistance in the Revolution.

In a statement dated 13 February 2024, the NUG condemned the military junta's activation of the Conscription Law and declared it unlawful. The NUG has not issued a specific policy regarding students who enrol in SAC universities to avoid the draft, only stressing the NUG's continued effort to promote participation in educational programmes that align with its democratic principles (rather than in those controlled by the military regime).

Ethnic post-secondary education offers

Ethnic education systems, in particular EAO schooling systems, have been described in detail in Lall (2021a); however, the coup has had two effects on these parallel systems. First, it has led to their massive expansion as families fleeing persecution in the urban areas arrived in EAO-controlled territories and enrolled their children in EAO schools, especially in Kayah and Karen States. Ethnic parents who had previously sent their children to government basic education schools also voted with their feet, switching to EAO provision. A vacuum in the education sector was created by CDM teachers leaving their jobs, initially and partially filled by EAO schools (Rinehart et al. 2024). These had long been sites of autonomy and resistance, but the coup has increased their relevance through what South et al. (2024) term a 'post-coup bottom-up federating process'. The second effect of the coup was that EAOs and ethnic nationality civil society leaders starting to develop tertiary education options. Some of these are briefly described next.[12]

It is important to recognise that tertiary education from EAO providers is not completely new. In the first instance, EAO schools have needed teachers and therefore the Mon, Karen and Kachin education systems have provided teacher training for many decades. The oldest EAO education department was established by the KNU in 1947 and their teacher training college established in 1958. As of 1997 the Karen

Teachers Working Group (KTWG) took charge of teaching quality and in 2004, the KTWG established the Karen Teacher Training College, which provides a two-year programme. The Kachin Independence Organisation (KIO) Education Department, created in 1978–9, established a Teacher Training School in 1997, which was upgraded to an Institute of Education in 2007–8. The Mon National Education Committee was established in 1992 as part of the New Mon State Party, although the Mon commitment to education goes back to the early 1970s, when community-supported teaching began in conflict-affected Mon areas. Mon teacher training developed as a part of the expansion of the Mon schooling system, which proceeded rapidly after the ceasefire in 1995 (Lall and South 2018). EAO-supported teacher training was usually taken up by young people – mostly women, who had completed their secondary schooling in one of the few secondary schools operated by their EAO.[13] Whilst teacher training was a normal part of the EAO education ecosystem, necessary to keep their language and culture alive, EAOs, with the exception of the KIA, which had developed some post-secondary options in agriculture, law and nursing in addition to their teacher training, did not provide a wide range of higher education courses.

The resumption of conflict seems to have been the main driver for the creation of higher education options by EAOs. The 1994 KIO ceasefire broke down in 2011. As a result, more than 100,000 IDPs fled to KIO-controlled territory – and they looked to the KIO to provide education for their children. The KIO schools gradually switched from teaching in Burmese to Kachin (Jingpaw) and English, slowly disengaging from the Myanmar government's system. Prior to 2011, KIO high school graduates had been able to matriculate at associated government schools and access higher education provided by the Myanmar government, largely because they had been following the government curriculum. However, in 2011 an order from the Myanmar government curtailed this practice. The result was that from 2011 onward, KIO school graduates were no longer able to join Myanmar government universities, even if they had been taught the government curriculum. This move prompted the KIO and other Kachin CBOs to expand Kachin Higher Education options for students matriculating from KIO schools (Lall 2021a). In 2011, existing Kachin HEIs included the Kachin Theological College and Seminary in Myitkyina, the Nursing College and the College of Agriculture in Laiza; the Federal Law College, the Institute of Education and the Intensive English Program, a graduate English programme (including literature), all in Mai Ja Yang (MJY). In 2013 the Liberal Arts College in MJY opened its doors. As shall be seen, their higher education offerings have continued to grow in the last decade.

The coup and the resulting civil war had a similar effect to the one experienced by the KIO a decade earlier on other EAOs, who have been striving to develop tertiary education for their ethnic nationality youth, who are no longer able or willing to access SAC-controlled higher education. At a January 2025 conference sponsored by the Myanmar Education Consortium in Bangkok, ethnic higher education providers described what had been achieved since the coup.

At the time of writing, the Kachin Education Consortium (KEC) manages five HEIs that have been developed into proper universities. The Institute of Education now also offers post-graduate master's programmes and other colleges provide diploma and bachelor programmes. The Kachin Higher Education Network was created in 2019 to accredit the courses of their colleges and universities and ensure quality.

There was no surprise that Kachin provision is the most advanced, having started earlier than higher education initiatives in other regions; however, the Karen Education and Culture Department (KECD) has become quite developed as well. At the time of writing, they boast 24 colleges, some of which are private and run by the church or other providers but which are linked in with the wider Karen higher education provision.

The Mon National Education Committee (MNEC) has also been busy developing higher education beyond its teacher training by creating the Mon National College in 2022. The college offers seven academic programmes including nursing, mass media, community leadership and management. Like other EAO education departments they are working to expand their offer and upgrade the course to bachelor's level. Support for the creation of the courses has come from links with Thai, UK and US universities, with students receiving scholarships to continue their studies as well as support from foreign academic staff for curriculum development.

The Southern Shan-based Restoration Council of Shan State (RCSS), an EAO that has not been known for an extensive network of primary schools, relying more on community schools with some RCSS-funded teachers, has likewise created a college (Lall et al. 2020). Loi Ta Leng College focuses on political science, with a priority on issues related to ethnic conflict and public policy. Students are able to study for a year at an affiliated Thai university and graduates are then expected to work for Shan CBOs focused on peace building and the wider development of their community. The college is working to expand its offer to include subjects relevant to their community such as agriculture, teacher training, public administration and international relations.

Another ethnic nationality tertiary education institution has been developed by the Karenni, who have established a centre with two colleges (Seh Theh College and the Karenni National College) offering GED training. The Demoso-based Seh Theh College was opened in 2021 but had to be moved after being bombed in 2023. They offer two majors (in education and community development) and aim to open courses in social science and information technology. The Karenni National College came about through a collaboration between Karenni Post Ten (KnPT) and Karenni Leadership Management Course (KNMC) and has existed since 2015. It grants diplomas in public health, computer science, social science and community development.

There have been recent efforts to develop tertiary education in Chin State in response to concerns that limited access to higher education could hinder long-term regional development.[14] Preparations are underway to establish a Chin National University, and pre-college programmes began in January 2025 with an initial cohort of 150 students. One of the respondents said, 'If we do not offer higher education, we fear our younger generation only know how to hold guns, but not be able to do any office work' (INT CS). However, significant challenges remain, including a shortage of teaching staff, textbooks, computers and library resources, as well as the need for dormitory facilities. Despite these obstacles, plans are in place to launch an undergraduate programme with two initial majors – IT and English – before expanding into 11 faculties.

It has become clear that many of those opposing the SAC have used the Revolution as a springboard to create new higher education systems. This includes EAOs and ethnic stakeholders, who seek to guarantee the survival of their own language and culture while making sure their youths have a future. As with the NUG education department, much of the focus is on teacher training and making sure the schooling system continues for the younger generation. Nevertheless, there has been a broadening of the higher education offer to include other courses, and the social sciences – viewed as catalysts of critical thinking – are set to play an important role.

In a revolution, who needs education?

As was seen in the previous chapter, there is a strong desire and need for post-secondary education across many different subjects. The next chapter will detail the views held by the students on the role of higher education in the Revolution, but the following section offers a few reflections on who needs education in the midst of a revolution. In the first instance, education is important for the fighters – being able to complete their education is particularly important for those who have taken up arms and joined the PDFs on the front lines.

> When I lived in the jungle in the armed Revolution, lots of kids had not even finished high school. Kids are in armed struggle and are soldiers. But all want education. All just want to go to school. They don't want to remain soldiers. Especially NUG needs a plan for these students to continue education even though they are in the armed struggle in the jungle. (FGD MS)

The logistics of making education available to revolutionary fighters or students on the run is challenging, not least because of lack of access to the internet and the constant risk of attacks.

> Implementing interim education is challenging, especially now, when internet connectivity is unreliable. However, once democracy is achieved, we anticipate improvements in living standards and higher education. (FGD MS)

Despite this student's hope that improved higher education would be achieved once the Revolution had succeeded, many realise that education is needed now as well. A student founder of SUM explained that

> Education is very important in the Revolution. Always need to offer educational opportunities, young people need options (opportunities) ... The education is also important for the young armed actors. Even the young revolutionaries need to continue education. The Revolution and education cannot separate, need to go together. (FGD MS)

The former academic who set up the institute focused on minority issues mentioned previously, and who wants to educate the youth of the Revolution in these matters, explains that working together against the common enemy and building inclusive structures through education is key to prepare for an inclusive post-coup Myanmar. Some student revolutionaries do not understand the issues posed by diversity; he expects that the same problems that divided Myanmar society before the coup will re-emerge, even if the Revolution wins, unless those at the forefront of the Revolution are educated.

> ... Education and Revolution are coming together. Now it's armed struggle. But there is also an ideological Revolution. They are trying to remove army from politics, the problems of the country will not be solved without solution of the ethnic problems and other minorities. People don't have the knowledge. (INT MS)

Increasing knowledge is therefore a crucial part of the Revolution; hence, higher education has to continue in whatever form is possible. Most students agree – they spoke about a system change and a mindset change. This is also the aim of the Revolution, and it cannot be achieved without education.

> The change in people's ideas and mindsets is crucial. It's about a fundamental shift in how they think and perceive things. (FGD MS)

> We anticipate that the military junta will fall within two years, allowing us to return home by 2024. However, it's important to recognise that the Revolution is not just a fight against the military junta; it's also a struggle against class inequality. (FGD MS)

During the November 2023 fieldwork in Thailand the students were increasingly optimistic that the SAC would fall in light of an EAO push against the Tatmadaw. They spoke about how the success of the Revolution depended on 'the change in people's ideas and mindsets' and therefore on education.

Conclusion and analysis: resistance through higher education

Early in the Revolution, the Myanmar Student Union took the stand that until the Revolution had been won and the SAC was removed from power, no student should continue their education. This position was endorsed by the NUG. Their view was that in order to change the country, everyone had to stop living their usual lives and make sacrifices for the Revolution. Students had a particular responsibility – it was inconceivable that certain students would give up everything they had, including their lives, whilst other would continue studying, even at universities not under SAC control – for example, at HEIs abroad. Respondents explained it as a form of fairness vis-à-vis those who had made the ultimate sacrifice. However, as the Revolution and the fight to remove the SAC has been ongoing, the NUG has revised its stance. Joining or rejoining an SAC university is still seen as a betrayal of the Revolution and all those sacrificing their lives for freedom. However, what the Spring Universities offer is an acceptable pathway forward. The same can be said of studying abroad, but the risk in this option is that students might not return if they believe they will not be able to survive once back in Myanmar. Online education provides an alternative way to access higher education for some, even if it doesn't reach everyone. Nevertheless, quality education is understood as key to resolving the country's shortage of professionals. Beyond the formation of qualified workers in the human capital sense, higher education is now also seen as essential in changing the Gramscian narrative of the country. The focus is therefore not only on the type of education that logically leads to particular jobs, but also on the social sciences per se, which can foster critical thinking and a better understanding of human rights. Throughout numerous conversations with respondents, higher education emerged as an essential pillar in the reconstruction of Myanmar and the building of the future country. In this context, the Spring Universities were very much viewed as part of the resistance.[15] This attitude, however, is limited to those who are actively part of the Revolution; those who wanted to sit out the conflict at home whilst others protested at the cost of their freedom or their lives, are seen as betraying the values of the Spring Revolution. The gap between CDM and non-CDM students and teachers/academics has become a difficult issue, especially in light of the SAC's conscription law – issues that will be discussed in the next chapter. In the meantime, the Spring Universities see for themselves a role much larger than just being a part of the Revolution. Until students can safely study in Myanmar again, these HEIs will continue working to provide education to those who need it. And once the students can go back, they intend to rebuild Myanmar's higher education system.

> If we lose the Revolution we will continue doing this from here to support students with their education. If we win, we will return and set up a formal institution. (SU INT CM)

The achievements of the Spring Universities show that revolutions can be fought in many ways. Taking control of the country's higher education by offering online courses and opening new possibilities to the younger generation in Myanmar has become an important way of resisting the SAC – one that is not easily shut down.[16] In many ways this is an example of Foucault's tactical reversal. By taking control of higher education, the SAC's hold on the universities is deligitimised; and as a group, the students who created the SUs are part of the youth network that Novelli et al. (2024) have described. But what the Spring Universities are doing is so much more. Returning to the theoretical framework, we can see that they are leading the intellectual resistance to the military regime. Their work underpins the change of narrative and mindset that all students agree is required for the long-term change of the country. Myanmar does not only need doctors and engineers. It needs critical thinkers who can imagine a new, inclusive and peaceful Myanmar that is able to delink from military rule. It needs young people invested in politics with an understanding of what it means to include all ethnic and religious groups. The leaders of the Spring Universities believe that higher education should be accessible to all, and that positive change can only happen if Myanmar's youth are both highly educated and share in this vision. In doing so they also resist the current neoliberal higher education narrative. In this respect, they are unique in their approach. Their resistance is to more than just the regime – it is also to the Western neoliberal education market's narrative.

The next chapter will look at how the students who are resisting the SAC understand the development of the Revolution, and how they view the role of higher education within the Revolution and in the future rebuilding of the country.

Notes

1 The University of Bologna was also created by students for students in 1088, which means that this is by no means the first time students have founded HEIs. However, it does seem to be the first time that forcibly displaced students have created such institutions for their peers – aided by the online tools that everyone started to use during the COVID-19 pandemic.

2 Originally, they also had funding from USAID.

3 This did not include those who might have returned to a SAC university.

4 See also Wong and Kareng (2023).

5 Prasse-Freeman and Sebro (2021) discuss how the coup has also fostered hopes for a more inclusive, pro-poor, trans-ethnic political movement that rejects both military rule and elitist liberal governance.

6 Discussion with United Nations University officials in Tokyo, summer 2025.

7 Ministry of Education. https://moe.nugmyanmar.org/en/.

8 This is, however, risky and has led to arrests of students who tried to use these certificates to continue their studies abroad. See Myanmar News Agency (2024) and RFA Burmese (2025b).

9 https://moe.nugmyanmar.org/en/.

10 The Spring Normal University maintains a website at https://snuedu.org/.

11 There exist other online universities that have links with the NUG, but we did not meet with them.

12 It should be noted that certain EAOs – in particular KNU and NMSP – have traditionally provided vital services for their communities, including education and healthcare. For an update on post-coup provision of such services, see South et al. (2023).

13 EAO schooling has been mostly provided at primary school level with children, especially in the Mon and Kachin areas, switching to government secondary provision before some attempted to access government higher education.

14 As the Chin group was not part of the Myanmar Education Consortium conference, this is based on personal interviews with individuals involved in education in Chin State in February 2025.

15 This also reflects Nick Cheesman's (2021) argument that the core threat to the military also lies in an alternative vision of sovereignty and governance, as well as the views of four CDM academics collected by Rahmat et al. (2025, p. 12), who explain how these academics 'now view education as a fundamental component of national reconstruction'.

16 The importance of the online space is also highlighted by Ryan et al. (2024), who examine how resistance actors used Facebook groups to build inter-ethnic solidarity post-coup and how digital platforms facilitated dialogue, empathy and coordination among divided communities.

5
Student views and voices on the Spring Revolution and the future of Myanmar

> 'The Spring Revolution is set to transform the lives of individuals in Myanmar. Having endured decades of military rule since the 1960s, the people experienced a glimpse of democracy between 2010 and 2021. This exposure to democratic governance highlighted the stark contrast with military rule, prompting many to participate in the Revolution.'

Myanmar students are not pursuing an education solely to learn, acquire knowledge and obtain a degree suitable for the job market, rather they seek a space that can support them in the process of living through the revolutionary experience and support a just Revolution in their country. As discussed in the previous chapters (in particular in Chapter 4 on the HEIs set up by students for their peers), being a student is at the core of their identity and higher education is a safe space they want to own and control. Gaining access to higher education is a way to delegitimise the Myanmar regime and prove that it cannot control their lives or the future of their country. The higher education they want for themselves and for Myanmar has to do with learning and acquiring knowledge, but also with resilience and resistance – it is the fundamental basis for the Revolution. This chapter engages with the voices of the students to shed light on how they conceive of the Revolution, and how they understand the role of higher education in the Revolution and in the future of Myanmar.

Defining the Revolution: what does it mean?

> On one morning everything disappeared. Everything we knew disappeared. (FGD MS)

The Revolution did not start off as such. Like most major political turning points in Myanmar's trajectory and in its people's lives, the momentous change that was about to befall the students was both unclear and unlikely when the tanks rolled up towards the parliament in Nay Pyi Taw. As discussed earlier, disagreements between General Min Aung Hlaing and Daw Aung San Suu Kyi about the elections had been rumbling on for a while. However, on that 1 February morning, as a fitness instructor was recording her workout routine on one of the large roundabouts of the capital, the unexpected military takeover took place in the background (BBC News 2021).

Students described their immense shock at the coup; they could not imagine that what had become normal over the last decade was about to be taken away. Their normal resembled that of most students today – coffee shops, mobile phones and the internet, student associations where politics were hotly debated, part-time jobs to make ends meet, dreams of a better future as they witnessed and contributed to the opening up and the development of their country. The new reality arrived gradually. It was the slow loss of daily comforts and necessities which led to the realisation that they had a responsibility to fight the return of the military dictatorship. This led to the growth of a wider movement. One of the respondents explained that students were initially not that interested in politics but concerned that their lives would change. It was at first a very selfish reaction. The realisation that they were heading back to the 1980s and 1990s, when their parents had suffered, was what transformed them from students into political activists and revolutionaries.

> Particularly at the initial phase, most of the young people taking part in the demonstration or strike are not based on political motives. They didn't really care about change in the political paradigm. They were concerned with losing their individual rights. First, they lost internet, then electricity, then they were not able to buy things. Glimpse of future is very dark, so they decided – let us be the generation to sacrifice ourselves for future generations. Only way is to take down military. We are against not only military but any dictator who will take away our rights. (SU FGD MS)

But it was also because their parents had suffered that the students say this time it was enough, and they were willing to sacrifice all they had, including their lives as the aforementioned quote explains. It was a radical departure from their ordinary existence and a jump into the unknown.

The concept of 'rights' as it is understood in Western society is a relatively recent development in Myanmar. A survey on citizenship at the start of the reform process in 2013 showed that young people did not expect much from the state; it was civil society that complemented or even provided many basic services related to health or education, especially in remote and conflict-affected areas (Lall et al. 2014). In urban areas, the middle classes that had emerged in the early 2000s chose to buy out and use private providers where possible. Some of these attitudes shifted during the reforms as the state, first under President Thein Sein and then under the NLD leadership, started to build up a social contract with its (urban) citizens, often with the help of international development partners, who financed reforms in education, healthcare and other administrative areas (Lall 2016). The reforms were accompanied by freedom of expression and freedom of movement. Students who entered the university a decade after the reforms began to have a sense of their rights, and this is what makes them different from the earlier generations. The coup took those rights away. Students expressed a variety of ways how they felt their individual rights were violated, and then how they transitioned to seeing that they had a larger responsibility towards their country. Some were prompted by the fact that they were losing their education – and, as a consequence, being robbed of their future.

> Most of the people who joined the Revolution did not do so because of pressure, they took their own decision. However, [what was important is that] people can't continue their education. (FGD MS)

Others felt the coup had violated them and the country.

> Before the coup the situation is stable, but after the coup [it changed]. The coup abused our rights. I am not from any organisation or party. But the coup abused all, so I became involved. (FGD MS)

> The coup destroyed our hopes and those of future generations. (INT IB)

Students described the Revolution mostly using the words '*change*', '*game changer*', or '*turning point*'. They explained how it had completely transformed their lives, how suddenly they felt responsible for '*fixing the big disaster*' by fighting against the dictatorship. At first this was defined by participating in the CDM. It is notable that at this point there was widespread hope that the military would hear them and the coup could be reversed. In retrospect, the reversal of the military takeover looks unlikely and the hope that their voices would be considered seems naive; however, just a decade prior President Thein Sein, a former general, had listened to demonstrations regarding the popular discontent with the Chinese-financed Myitsone Dam in Kachin State (Chan 2024). Hence, young people really believed that their voices would be heard, and for many days the demonstrations were completely peaceful, even resembling street parties, as described in Chapter 1. It was only when the military used force and started to shoot into the crowds that a there was a gradual realisation that peaceful resistance would not yield the desired results. For a few days (or possibly even weeks), students had hoped that by continuing their protests on the street, and by remaining peaceful themselves, the international community would intervene. Protests in front of UN Agency Headquarters with signs in English testified to the trust that the protesters had placed in foreign powers, who they believed would protect them and protect Myanmar's reforms – which had, in effect, been financed by Western donors (Christian Science Monitor Editorial Board 2021). When it became clear that no one would come to their aid, there was a widespread sense of disbelief and a feeling of abandonment. It was almost a betrayal – Western powers had supported the reforms and Western agencies had established themselves in Myanmar, but when things got tough these same Western agencies and their foreign employees simply vanished. As the realisation that they were on their own dawned on them, some students left to take up arms, getting combat training on the border, and founding and joining the PDFs (University World News 2021). Others started supporting the NUG and PDFs financially by fundraising (for example, by playing digital games to raise money) (Slow 2023). Some spoke about how they were documenting human rights violations and war crimes, collecting evidence for the International Court of Justice. There was a strong sense that one day these crimes would have to be accounted for.

> People are participating in the Spring Revolution in three ways: through civil disobedience movements (CDM), strikes and armed

> Revolution, each contributing as much as they can. Despite facing significant challenges, the entire country remains actively engaged in the Revolution. (FGD MS)

There was an increased realisation that the military had always sought to control people's lives, repressing any and all who did not fit into their definition of being Myanmar.

> The military is always same as long ago and bad. After the transition period – fake partial democracy. But we see what is the difference. Right now, there are abuses on religion and LGBT rights; before [there was] racism [and] media censorship. (FGD MS)

The same student credited the decade of 'fake partial democracy' with having opened their eyes. They believed that

> ... the Spring Revolution is set to transform the lives of individuals in Myanmar. Having endured decades of military rule since the 1960s, the people experienced a glimpse of democracy between 2010 and 2021. This exposure to democratic governance highlighted the stark contrast with military rule, prompting many to participate in the Revolution ... (FGD MS)

Many respondents acknowledged that this fight had already been going on in the ethnic areas and that the ethnic groups had been fighting for their self-determination for a long time. This was not something that they had understood or cared about previously. Only after the military started to use the same tactics against them did they understand the plight of the ethnic groups. The students detailed how the military had controlled the country's resources and oppressed its people for decades. Still, the wider public did not get involved until the conflict affected those in central Myanmar and the military began to shoot student demonstrators with live ammunition.

> The Revolution has long been active in ethnic areas, but this time, the Bamar people are also involved. What I want to emphasise is that the root cause of the problem is the military junta. (FGD MS)
>
> Before the Spring Revolution, warfare was confined to areas outside central Burma. However, the conflict has now spread across the entire country. This widespread engagement signifies a unified

understanding among the populace of the junta's malevolence, leading to a collective resistance. (FGD MS)

The students say the coup led to an *'awakening'*, or *'shift in mindset'* that unified the whole country, not only in the fight against the military takeover in Myanmar but against all forms of dictatorships.

> This Revolution is not just a response to the military coup against the elected government; it represents a shift in the mindset of the Myanmar people. It's a stand against all dictators. (FGD MS)

This coming together holds profound significance in Myanmar, where for centuries ethnic and religious faultlines have divided society, and where first the British colonial administration, and later the Tatmadaw, used ethnic and religious divisions to create a hierarchy of identities and rule. Participants were clear that the Revolution went beyond the NLD or the NLD-dominated NUG. This ideological shift, which goes beyond what the NUG represents as a shadow government, is one element that is completely different from previous student uprisings against military rule. In the 1980s, the NLD used to proclaim that the main aim of the resistance was democracy and that ethnic grievances could be dealt with once democracy had been achieved. Today's student revolutionaries proclaim that overcoming ethnic and religious faultlines is a key part of the Revolution, the basis on which to build a new country.[1] The feeling of a new 'righteousness' – both vis-à-vis the military and their parents' generation – was palpable in all discussions. It drove students to say that they would win, had to win, because they were right – more right than any generation that had come before.

> We are going to win because we believe. We are participating in the Revolution because we are standing on the right side, justice. (FGD MS)

There were early hopes that the Revolution would be concluded in a matter of months or perhaps a couple of years. However, as one student explained, the Revolution was taking *'longer than expected'* (SU FGD MS). The next section discusses how the students see the progress of the Revolution and how things have changed for them since the coup.

The progress of the Revolution

Post-coup societal protest was initially conceived in non-violent terms. As described previously, civil disobedience was seen as the best way to counter the military takeover. The starting point was non-violence. This meant giving up jobs (and for many government employees, also housing). The sacrifices were immense, especially for the government employees who lost their salaries and whose families were thrown out of their government apartments. It was only when soldiers started to shoot innocent protestors that those countering the coup realised that CDM had proved insufficient. This led to the growth of a revolutionary movement, which in today's terms includes the kinds of protests meant to disrupt the governing of the country. These range from school boycotts and not paying taxes to taking part in the raging armed conflict between EAOs/PDFs and the Tatmadaw. Many respondents said they had not wanted armed conflict.

> We joined CDM, wanted to do non-violence against the coup. People are very poor and oppressed for many decades. This Revolution cannot end only with CDM. Now [there is] armed conflict. [This] Means more orphans. More people are being killed. We didn't want to see this kind of armed conflict. We wanted to build a democratic federal country. Junta didn't give respect to the diversity of the country. People didn't enjoy the human rights. We want to have protection of human rights. (SU FGD CM)

The development of the armed resistance is multifaceted (Ye Myo Hein 2024) and its details are beyond the aims of this book, which focuses on student voices and student views of the Revolution. As detailed in Chapter 3, some students went to the border to learn urban resistance skills from EAOs, and some went to get combat training. Those with explosives skills returned to the urban areas to target government buildings, including schools. Yangon in particular experienced numerous attacks over a period of many months.[2] Others who had received combat training either joined the EAOs or set up PDFs themselves. The collaboration between the PDFs and the EAOs is complex, and not all EAOs are fighting the Tatmadaw with the same aims as the PDFs. For some EAOs (such as the SSPP,[3] UWSA[4] and AA[5]), this Revolution is a fight between Bamars with little relevance to them. Other EAOs (such as the KNU,[6] the KNPP[7] and the KIA[8]) see the conflict as their one big chance to remove the military from power and politics, and they are broadly on the same side as the wider revolutionary movement. Ironically, it is the group of EAOs least aligned with the Spring Revolution – the Three Brotherhood Alliance[9] – that has most helped the advances of the PDFs. Despite the high cost of lives over months of fighting, students were much more hopeful after Operation 1027, as they saw the Tatmadaw in retreat from multiple parts of Myanmar.

On 27 October 2023, after the battle of Laukkai, the three EAOs launched a surprise operation against the Tatmadaw and successfully took control of the Kokang Self-Administered Zone. This was followed by further offensives in Rakhine State, Shan State, Chin State, Kayah State and Sagaing Region, liberating more towns and severely weakening the Tatmadaw's position.[10]

> If the current situation continues in Myanmar we will win. This is not only about freedom but also about standing up for truth and people to know their rights and shout for it. (FGD MS)

The conflict has come at a high cost to civilians, who are regularly targeted by the military. Any area that has been 'liberated' is at risk of air strikes and other punitive actions by the Tatmadaw, which has treated anyone they suspect of sympathising with the NUG and the resistance with unspeakable cruelty (Fauldner 2024). Some respondents explained that the inhabitants of conflict-affected areas had to evacuate regularly but were still hopeful that the Revolution would win.

> They are not demotivated, unlike those in Yangon. As those people don't lose hope, we have a shot to win. People in conflict area are more hopeful than those on urban areas. (SU FGD CM)

When asked how they saw the progress of the Revolution, students said confidently '*We will win*'. And what does it mean to win? Others answered – '*not giving up*' (FGD MS).

> [This is a] slow and long battle. I don't think the youth will ever give up. The youth will not stop till they win or have the upper hand. It's so much better than before with technology and youth and all age groups. It's not a battle that will end and give up. (FGD MS)

> We will not just raise the white flag and give up. We will never bow back down to the military. (FGD MS)

> Not winning doesn't mean losing, it has been going on for 80 years. This will go on forever. There will still be ethnic groups fighting. The crisis will go on for a long time. We need to provide help for those who are resisting the military until victory is achieved. (FGD MS)

Despite all the death and destruction none of our respondents spoke of the sacrifices being made. And real, personal sacrifices are being made – all respondents had lost loved ones, some had bullet wounds, female fighters who had been arrested had experienced sexual abuse, and in the hospital in Mae Sot, students were undergoing amputations. 'Revolutionaries are not calculating resources, they believe in what they are doing' (FGD MS). Failure was not seen as an option – 'If it fails we keep fighting. We fail only when we give up' (FGD MS).

Few of those who took part in the FGD envisaged the possibility that they might not win; the sense of responsibility to change the country and the future of all citizens was paramount. '*This Revolution can change the future for all individuals in Myanmar. Every possibility can happen – people can win or SAC can win. But we need to win.*' (FGD MS)

Across all respondents there was a widespread belief that the SAC would not survive. In that sense, the Revolution would be successful. There was also widespread agreement that defeating the SAC (or the SAC falling on its own) might constitute some sort of victory, but was not the end of the road.

> The falling of Min Aung Hlaing does not mean victory. Victory requires complete social change. Now the fighting is leading in the Revolution. Politics has been left behind. Priority is fighting war. There is no agreed political framework. There is no agreed constitution. (INT MS)

Two main themes emerged – what kind of a country Myanmar would and should become once the Revolution was successful, and the worry that after the common enemy had been removed, the revolutionary forces would fall apart and possibly even come into conflict with each other. Already different armed groups, some EAOs and various PDFs were in conflict with one another about controlling territory and villages. The NUG has not been in a position to control the PDFs, even those operating under its banner; it has had even less influence over the EAOs, many of which have been at war with the Myanmar military for decades. At the time of writing the Myanmar map looks like a series of territories controlled by many different groups, with a localised devolved governance structure in certain places (Figure 2.1; International Institute for Strategic Studies n.d.). There is no centralised government that is able to rule adequately. Many respondents mentioned the power vacuum, with some saying that there was already such a vacuum and that the NUG did not have the capacity to fill it.

> [It is] clear now that the military will collapse sooner or later. The problem will be the power vacuum and how we build unity when the military goes down. The NUG has not done well in building unity with ethnic groups. Military will collapse but will we become a federal democratic country? That's not sure. (FGD MS)

For a true federal democracy to emerge, Myanmar needs unity amidst its diversity. It also needs political leadership. These challenges will now be discussed.

Unity

As has been mentioned, what emerged from the discussions was that Bamar students now felt a greater empathy and understanding for the ethnic groups and what they had suffered under the military in the decades since the country had won its independence. The need for solidarity and unity across ethnic divides was a reoccurring theme, reflecting what the founder of the Minority Affairs Institute – cited in the previous chapter – had explained.[11] However, students were worried that those in positions of responsibility might not understand this.

> [We] need common political objectives for the country. Generation Z wants to negotiate with minority groups, participation of all the stakeholders. NUG is offering parallel commitment in health, education and social needs. (FGD MS)

> The duration [of the Revolution] will not be extended if we remain united. It's more about the extent of people's involvement rather than when it will end. (FGD MS)

It is also unclear if the importance of unity and solidarity is understood more widely, or if these are priorities driven solely by the need to fight the Tatmadaw. Walton and Aye Thein (2023) discuss how, despite the opportunities for new alliances between Bamar-majority protestors and long-standing EAOs, these remain tentative and fraught with mistrust. As has already been stated, the aims of EAOs and Bamar revolutionaries do differ. The ethno-national framing of divisions also means that even in resistance circles, the systemic exclusion of unofficial ethnic minorities persists (Aung Ko Ko et al. 2024). It needs to be remembered that despite the reforms, this generation was educated in Bamar-centric schools with Bamar-centric textbooks and teachers (Lall 2021a). Informal conversations with student members of PDFs after the formal FGDs revealed that they believed they had the right to live in and use ethnic areas for shelter until the defeat of the military in the Bamar heartlands. A united vision shared by all was assumed and the views of the EAOs or the ethnic people were not considered, reflecting the traditional hierarchical nature of inter-ethnic relations in Myanmar. Conversely, it is unknown how the ethnic youth feel about unity. EAOs have been fighting for a measure of autonomy, or in certain cases independence – some, like the KNU, since 1948. While the youth across Karen, Kayah, Chin and Kachin are supporting the Spring Revolution, they might have very different views on what outcome would be beneficial for their people.[12] Most of the respondents who took part in our research were Bamar youths from urban areas, and only a few were of ethnic nationality, which means that the understanding of unity discussed here is limited.

The future of the country

Students were particularly worried about who would lead the country in the future. Even those directly allied with the NUG through their organisation did not believe that the NUG had an automatic right to power. The NLD had been elected, but the coup had changed everything. They felt that the blood that was being spilt to reclaim freedom and the sacrifices they and their families had made allowed them to imagine a new country beyond one that was divided between the Tatmadaw and the NLD. This contrasts sharply with the view of some NUG representatives, who believe in the right of the NUG to form the government as soon as the Tatmadaw is defeated or removed and that the government in waiting was in effect the legitimate government of the country. This is not a position many students agreed with. Some spoke about the need for technical know-how to re-establish a working government and stated that politicians were '*not enough*'. They pointed out that politicians were only recognised if they had been '*political prisoners*', and neither the traditional politicians nor the political prisoners would have the required knowledge to rebuild and develop the country. Respondents talked about the need for a transitional justice system and observed that it would be complicated to set up; they spoke about societal change and the challenges of development.

> Because of coup many people lost families, jobs, home. They need healing and recovery. Support is needed. All the military government system is broken. Need to establish a new system for the country. (FGD MS)

> Despite numerous conflicts and victories by revolutionary forces, numerous challenges persist. The time required for combat is limited, but rebuilding the country will take much longer. We face issues such as homelessness, unemployment and loss of family members, all of which require recovery efforts. A new bureaucratic system is essential. (FGD MS)

Education was therefore essential, especially for the generation that was going to have to rebuild Myanmar in the future. The students explained that it was important to have educated people leading the country, rather than those with a history as political prisoners. The former academic who had set up the institute focusing on minority issues (discussed in the previous chapter) explained that education was important, especially for the young revolutionary soldiers. While there were some barriers, such as lack of internet access or restrictions on phone use, those who had fought and interrupted their education for the Revolution needed to be educated so that they could help rebuild the country. Their education had to focus on unity and equity. He recognised the challenge of preserving unity – but also the problem of explaining the actual meaning of unity to the mainly Bamar PDF fighters. Therefore, this interim period needed to be used to develop an inclusive education policy and system, both despite and because of the conflict. This needed to include minority students and disabled students, those who had been discriminated against by the regime. He felt there was a need to recognise the barriers to education and remove them, including the trauma faced by the young people fighting the war.

Across the board there was agreement that even when the conflict side of the Revolution concluded, building democracy and eradicating totalitarianism would not happen overnight and would not be easy, as can be seen in the following quotations:

> The Revolution will conclude soon. However, the ideological and cultural aspects of the Revolution will continue. (FGD MS)

> I perceive the Revolution against the military junta, along with revolutions against other dictatorships, as occurring concurrently in this era. (FGD MS)

> The Revolution won't be complete just by overthrowing the military. Although the SAC may weaken, it still holds significant power. Eradicating all forms of dictatorship, not just the SAC, will take time. Building democracy will also require time. (FGD MS)

The future they imagined was by no means guaranteed and would take time and work. The key thing was that it would be completely different from what Myanmar had been before. '*The Spring Revolution is not regime change – it's a system change*' (FGD MS). It was imagining this future and the system change they would build that kept them motivated. The need for higher education and the role it would play in this will now be discussed.

The role of higher education in the Revolution

Throughout the conversations with the students, higher education was identified as a key factor in the Revolution. In the FGDs, when asked about higher education, students shouted out that '*to build a good country, [you] need educated people*'; '*Higher education can open everyone's eyes. Need a lot of technicians in the future, lawyers, doctors. For that we need higher education*'; '*Everyone should get higher education when we are reconstructing*' (FGDs MS and CM).

As already discussed above, being a student is a core part of the identity of those leading the Revolution. They are the ones who were involved in the protests and the armed resistance, and they are the ones sacrificing their lives for a changed country and what they believe will be a brighter future for the next generation. In their minds, education, being a student and the Revolution cannot be separated. One student leader who is part of the alternative institutions that have been set up quoted Che Guevara – '*if you want to do a Revolution you need to be educated*' (INT MS).

Historically, as discussed by Licia Proserpio (2025) in her volume on Myanmar higher education, political resistance was very much part of being a student in Myanmar. This was, however, not the case during the reform period, where students became much less political. As explained by a student leader and founder of one of the student-led HEIs, over the last decade there were two groups of students within the Students' Union, but '*only around 10 per cent were politically engaged – the others were concerned about personal rights, but not the future of the country. After the coup this changed, and many more students became politically engaged by resisting the coup'* (SU INT MS). The students' unions from across Myanmar created a Revolutionary Council (SURC) to represent the collective voice of students. The SURC has created a youth policy, a gender policy and they are represented at the NUG and on the General Strike Committee. As armed resistance has increased, the SURC has become less active. However, the increased politicisation of students both inside Myanmar and on the border is undeniable.

Discussions of the role of higher education in the Revolution led to three different themes – the poor education received under the military, resulting in a knowledge gap that needed to be filled; the Revolution as a means to regain the right to education after the destruction of the universities; and the role of the NUG and shadow institutions as interim solutions.

The knowledge gap

Students explained passionately that the higher education they had received under the military government – the same government that ended up destroying the universities during the coup – was substandard.

> Teachers did not allow to give a in-depth lectures. Even the political science course offered in Yangon University draws on the military junta. Thus, students have only limited knowledge about political science. (INT MS)

Because teachers were restricted in what they were allowed to teach, the respondent believed that most students don't understand politics. But it's not just about understanding politics – students complained that what they had learnt was basically worthless.

> The education system in Myanmar is nothing, I didn't have the chance to take the metric examination. In MS I took GED classes and realised that Myanmar certificates are worthless. You can't join higher education abroad. (FGD MS)

> We need to reform. In the old higher education system [students] only learn about the things in the textbooks. Skipping class. This has to be changed. (FGD MS)

There was some acknowledgement that the reforms in the decade prior to the Revolution had made a difference. A former lecturer at the university of foreign languages, who had participated in the education reform, saw no hope for higher education after the coup.

> We were only able to breathe between 2015–20. We experienced democracy briefly. I had hoped that the higher education sector could be transformed during reforms. I worked for NAQAC and for UNESCO. […] When the coup happened, there was no hope for higher education. (INT MS)

It is this loss of opportunity, the loss of a future that brings us to the second theme – taking back the right to education.

Taking back the right to education

Over many decades of military rule, rights have not been underpinning Myanmar's social contract due to military governance. However, the decade of reforms (Lall 2016) did give students a glimpse of what it meant to have rights, and this galvanised many students to fight against the military coup as their rights were taken away from them (Proserpio 2025). Respondents explained it thus:

> We have experience of liberalisation before [20]21, higher education is turning point […]. Students from higher education are leading the Revolution since the member of parliament didn't know what to do. Students feel junta take their rights. Students started [the Revolution] because they felt they had no future. PDF are not rebels. They are educated people who are fighting because they don't have choice. (SU FGD MS)

The note that the MPs didn't know what to do is telling – and reflects the earlier point that the NUG did not have an automatic right to power at the end of the conflict.

> We are fighting this Revolution to get back our educational rights and opportunities. Since the coup happened, many can't go abroad to study, that's what keeps the students motivated. If we don't fight and leave it, we will remain stuck under the military. No one wants to continue their educational journey under the junta. (FGD MS)

This student movement has developed into a different from of resistance from that of 1988 and 1990, when students were protesting against military rule without having experienced any form of liberalisation. This generation had realised that education opportunities were completely different when the country was under civilian control.

> Higher education is related with the Revolution. Under the military the education system is very bad, no one cares about higher education system under the junta. We are involved because we are students – we have a right to education. Under SPDC there were no scholarships. However, after the transition, the students had more opportunities. Thus, education opportunities are linked to democracy. (FGD MS)

The link between democracy and educational opportunities (or even rights more broadly) was a key realisation. Previous generations might have had access to education, even higher education, but not the kind that would lead to meaningful professional opportunities or the development of the country. Those who have created alternative education platforms (Chapter 4) think about the right to education at both the policy level (e.g. discussing a federal education charter that reflects devolved universities with new academic values) and the implementation level – that is, they think about how to provide the '*right of better education*' to all. As should be clear by now, this rights-based framing not only counters the hegemony of the military in Myanmar's education space but also runs contrary to the international neoliberal trend that has engulfed the region through standard education reforms.

There is much ongoing debate, however, about how to compensate those who sacrificed their spot in the university for the sake of the Revolution: '*Perhaps we can provide reparations for those who have lost their future because of the Revolution*' (FGD MS). It reflects the debate about the role of CDM (discussed further subsequently). The relevant question is the same: how should society repay those who gave up their higher education to support the Revolution?

These reflections and the realisation that a victorious end to the Revolution is still some way off have led students to rely on interim higher education solutions. If higher education is an important part of the Revolution, it becomes a crucial building block in reconstructing the country, as discussed in the next section.

The role of higher education in the future of post-coup Myanmar

> Education should be a tool for liberation, both during and after the Revolution. Junta are using education as a tool for oppression. Revolutionaries need to bring sympathy, empathy through education. (SU FGD CM)

It has become clear from the previous discussion that education – and particularly higher education – is the glue that joins the Revolution and the future of Myanmar as a new country. Everyone agreed that higher education is important in preparing for post-coup Myanmar.

A founder of one student-led HEI explained that beyond the classroom, higher education would play a role in effective policy formulation and that experts and professors would need to take part in the nation building process. International support to help the NUG develop higher education was also seen as important. Other respondents focused on the role of universities in teaching and learning. Many mentioned that the social sciences – actively discouraged by the military governments over decades – would be more important than ever. Values taught through higher education were also seen as vital to building the new country. As one founder of a student-led HEI explained

> Values and attitude are more important than knowledge and skills. Can see this concept through the example of non-CDM professor like [name withheld] who has knowledge and skill but not values. [We] need attitude and values. These are not given by the junta. It's difficult to deliver this. But the openness 2015–20 students had values and attitudes which is why they fight against the junta. (SU FGD CM)

Students mentioned that in the past, Myanmar students had obtained degrees but had not taken jobs related to their qualifications. They stated that the new higher education system needed to be relevant for their future employment. As Lall (2021a) observed, Myanmar has many medical doctors but very few of them actually practice medicine. One student explained that higher education needed to move away from central control and

> ... produce professionals that the country needs. So we can have federal democratic country. [...] In 2013 Thein Sein opened [HEIs]

> to foreign universities for training. In 2017 HR law training started with an elective. In 2019 mandatory course. Erasmus course on forced migration started in 2019 at Mandalay University leading project involving six countries. But the coup happened shortly after. (FGD CM)

For the country to move forward, the higher education learning and teaching environment would have to base itself on research and critical inquiry.

> The whole education system will go through biggest change. Will become practice and research based. Those in the battalion in the jungle using drones are now regretting they didn't have practice-based education. (FGD MS)

One student, however, cautioned that '*[w]e should not abolish everything in the old system. There were good systems in ancient times. Have to mix with new systems. [The aim is to] create educated people*' (FGD MS).

As a former professor of Yangon University reminded us, for Myanmar's future higher education to be inclusive, both access and quality needed to be reviewed. The SAC had focused on access, but the departure of CDM staff led to a reduction of quality with more junior staff appointed to senior positions (Proserpio 2025). Whilst issues of accreditation and recognition could be sorted out later, making sure that the education received was of high quality was a priority. The professor explained that the education system had to underpin the new federal union and that the focus needed to be on the reduction of hatred: '*Do not politicise the education. Do not forget SAC always politicise the education*' (INT MS). And whilst most are advocating for a future without discrimination, the higher education sector is more divided than ever on the issue of CDMers vs. non-CDMers. This debate has been ongoing. Even with the victory of the Revolution far from assured, those who joined the CDM and sacrificed their lives are advocating a reparations process for themselves as well as some form of punishment for those who did not (Frontier Myanmar 2023).

The conflict around CDM

Higher education in Myanmar has been fraught with disagreements over the years, and this is the latest conflict. It is inherently political and shows how hard it will be to follow the advice of the professor cited previously. The coup has caused what seems today to be an unbridgeable divide between the CDM and non-CDM participants. A study by Nyan Lynn Thit Analytica (2022b) surveyed both civil servants who had continued to work after the coup, and civil servants who had joined CDM, documenting the growing animosity of those who had made sacrifices towards those who had not. According to the survey, half of those who were not part of the CDM movement one year after the coup had actually left their jobs initially. However, due to threats to their families or the need to feed their families, they had returned to work. Many of them were sympathetic to the CDMers and despised the military government, but their personal circumstances did not allow them to actively join the Revolution. One of Nyan Lynn Thit's respondents wrote 'Although I can happily accept the punishments from the humane government in the post-Revolution period, I am more worried about the threats from the military towards my family and myself to go back to the workplace' (Nyan Lynn Thit Analytica 2022b, p. 14).

From the CDM side there was little sympathy. Students explained '*CDM vs non-CDM – how will they work together? Who will lose their job? Also issue with CDM and non-CDM students, how will they finish their degrees?*' (FGDs MS). This new faultline has the potential to further divide Myanmar. The issue is about sacrifice: who was willing to sacrifice what for the future of the country? And who is either a traitor or a free rider? The judgement heaped upon non-CDMers is severe, as the following quote shows:

> CDMers hope to become a democratic nation and have a federal education system. They love the truth and want to leave the military government. They have no wish to stay long with fear under the junta. They want to get freedom from fear and hope to create a better teacher education system with qualified and democratic leaders. Alternatively, non-CDMers are different from CDMers because those who keep working under the military government want to stay their lives with ease and comfort. They do not have the sense to differentiate what is right or wrong. (TE-AM cited in Khaing Phyu Htut et al. 2022)

While CDMers have been punished by the government, some non-CDMers have been targeted by the PDFs and the Ethnic Revolutionary Organisations (EROs) for not joining the CDM. According to Nyan Lynn Thit Analytica (2022b), 13 civil servants who continued working have been killed by the PDFs and EROs.[13]

The NUG made several announcements warning civil servants who had continued working to quit their jobs. On 4 February 2022, the NUG announced that action will be taken against non-CDM staff from the military-controlled Siyin Township administration to ensure that appropriate punishments were meted out.[14] With regard to higher education, the NUG official position is that when the country is rebuilt after the Revolution, CDM students would face more difficulties than non-CDM students due to the interruption in their education. Consequently, the NUG wants to create a quota for system for CDM students, not only with regard to employment but also political participation, so that they would be rewarded with welfare and job security for their sacrifices. As one NUG representative explained: '*Like quotas for women ... More prioritise to CDM students in future rather than opportunities to non-CDM*' (INT MS). They favour a policy that recommends even the private sector consider the 'special situation' of CDMers and give them priority. There is only limited sympathy for anyone who returned to an SAC university for reasons other than support of the SAC. One founder of a SU-led HEI explained the wider problem:

> Those who went back to university recently don't necessarily support the junta. More are returning but much less than before the coup. There are issues also with job opportunities. There is some understanding that they move on with their life. (SU FGD MS)

The two groups are increasingly viewed in black-and-white terms as opponents. The reality is more complex: after all, not all non-CDMers are supportive of the military and its government.[15] The enforcement of the conscription law in February 2024 – activated in light of unexpectedly high SAC losses – has made this point ever more salient. Under the law, all men between the ages of 18 and 35 and all women between the ages of 18 and 27 can be called up to serve for at least two years. The age range is wider for medical personnel. This law, which was written into the 2010 Constitution but not implemented until 2024, sent shockwaves through the student communities that had decided to stay in Myanmar, with some returning to SAC-controlled universities and others boycotting military-controlled higher education but not wanting to risk their lives in combat. The call up has meant that young people in that age range who would have liked to avoid fighting now know they will have to take up arms. Many opt to join PDFs and flee to EAO-controlled areas rather than join the Tatmadaw (Nai Aue Mon and Quadrini 2024). But given that they have waited until now (and are thus considered different from the CDMers who resisted the coup from the start), they are not always well received by long-term participants in the resistance.

Another part of the discussion on reparations has engaged with the costs paid by students living in conflict zones who were becoming poor and had lost the motivation to study and society's moral debt to them.

> [We] will have to do reparations for the people who have lost access. And demolish old health and education systems. Make changes. Will take time. But good for the future. (FGD MS)

> We have a significant responsibility to assist those who have lost access to education. While abolishing the old education system may take time, it's a worthwhile endeavour for the future. Looking ahead, there will be a stronger link between education and job opportunities, enhancing life prospects for many. Additionally, the roles of social scientists and anthropologists will become more prominent and influential in the future. (FGD MS)

These quotes show that the students engaged in the Revolution feel they have a heavy responsibility for the future of their country. They also shed light on students' attitudes towards their sacrifices and the righteousness of their choices.

Whither Myanmar?

Most of the student respondents for this book have been and still are actively involved in the Revolution, and a majority of those are on the Thai–Myanmar border working either as educational activists or as a part of the PDFs. They know what they are fighting for and what they want their country to become. Most have a positive outlook on the future, even if this future feels quite far away. These representatives of Gen Z were strong, mostly optimistic and highly driven. To provide balance to this picture, 31 other students who had left Myanmar and the border were interviewed. These students had the privilege of having received an EU-funded 'top-up' scholarship (EMPM) which allowed them to finish their degrees in another ASEAN university. This means that they all spoke sufficient English to study abroad, and all online interviews were conducted in English.[16] Some had already left Myanmar before receiving the scholarship, including a handful who were on the Thai border. However, the majority of these students had stayed in Myanmar after the coup, wanting to ride out the storm, hoping to resume their studies when conflict had passed. They were sympathetic to the CDMers, but not necessarily part of the revolutionary movement. They came from all walks of life, some from Yangon, others from smaller places in the Irrawaddy Delta, Mandalay Region and Shan State with parents ranging from shopkeepers, farmers and taxi drivers to lawyers and teachers. Most were Bamar and Buddhist, but the sample also included Chin, Rakhine, Karen and Mon, as well as a few Christians and one Muslim student. These students were more divided in their views of what the future held for their country, and many had a more negative outlook towards the future than the more active revolutionaries on the border. They were, however, united in their intention to want to return to the country and help rebuild whenever possible.

The future is bleak

> A lot has been destroyed it will take long to rebuild. Most people go abroad, even though they have the desire to contribute to the country. They don't have enough power. NUG – there are also conflicts. Even after the Revolution – who will govern our country? There needs to be a federal country with minority rights. For 16–18 years old they are still in Myanmar, normal people are stuck in Myanmar, they don't have money and they go to government schools and they are brainwashed. The future is in the hands of the youth, but they are being brainwashed. (OL INT)

This quote shows that those engaged in the Revolution might be ordinary Myanmar citizens choosing an extraordinary path, but that the majority of Myanmar citizens are still stuck under the military, which continues to use education to control the citizens' mindset. A former teacher, now studying abroad, pointed out that '*major cities are still under the military*'. Whilst she wants the students inside Myanmar to continue their education, she worries about the difference between rich and poor students. Students from rich families might be able to buy their way out of the military education, others would just leave school to become general workers and would not have a future.

Respondents pointed to issues rarely discussed by the revolutionary students, relating to the divisions within the NUG and other anti-military forces. There were many voices that had doubts about the NUG – '*lots of weaknesses, [but also] military side there are lots of challenges*'. Respondents acknowledged that the conflict could be ongoing, as armed groups were using the situation in the country to serve their own purpose – one spoke of a '*warlord mentality*' and another noted that '*too many groups were fighting for power*'. In fact, in certain EAO-controlled areas positive changes could be seen – '*I can see changes in Rakhine due to the EAO that are winning, but for the country I cannot see changes*'. In part, this is because seasoned armed groups already have administrative structures to serve their ethnic 'citizens' and those who live in their areas. This is particularly the case in Kachin State, where there is a functioning education system that goes from the primary level to post-secondary colleges (Lall 2021a). On the one hand, the conflict with the Tatmadaw made running the country more difficult for non-SAC forces. On the other, with Tatmadaw troops engaged around the country, certain areas under EAO control are now operating almost like independent countries. But the hope in these areas does not translate to those who see the wider conflict engulfing their country, with dozens of armed groups – both ethnic and PDFs – fighting and civilians getting caught in the middle. Some students also mentioned that if and when the conflict stopped, the pathway to developing the country would be long.

> I see no improvement happening. We all do not know. Even if things go back to normal, we need to develop our country, this will take a long time. (OL INT)

Some respondents complained that the conflict was impossible to follow, things were complicated and changed too rapidly: '*... everything is getting worse and it is not safe*'. Many said they just wanted their country back and that it was impossible to see what would happen because '*things are rapidly changing now*'. A few students were visibly hopeless: '*we cannot do anything. I have no hope*'. Others just thought it would take time: '*It will be not an easy pathway. It will take time. It is a very sad story. I don't see democracy in a short time*'. As shall be seen, time – and how much time will be required – is at the heart of much of the discussions.

The outcome will be good – but it will take time

Those who were optimistic about the future explained that it would take a long time to see positive change. '*In 20–30 years if we have enough effort, the future may be good*'; '*It will take a long time to see Myanmar go back at it was in 2015–20. Democracy will take time to be back*'. But the length of time respondents thought it would take varied significantly. Some believed it would take a generation. Others expected two or three more years would be enough.

> It is very hard to predict the future of our country. After three years of Revolution I am not satisfied with our progress. Hopefully, I think that by the time I graduate there may be some changes. (OL INT)

> I think within three years we will see the president we voted for returning. All the military will come down. Two years later we will return to Myanmar and rebuild our country. Things will definitely get better. Maybe also longer than two years, but it can only get better. (OL INT)

Only one respondent mentioned that a negotiation to find a peaceful solution would be better for the country, but that no leaders were capable of doing this.

> Maybe it will take longer than people expect to get a good result. If there can be a negotiation – peaceful – it would be better but I don't think the leaders can do this kind of peaceful negotiation – but would be better for our country. (OL INT)

Youth responsibility and going abroad

Another theme that emerged during the discussions was that of youth responsibility. One respondent said she had returned to study in order to support the future of Myanmar.

> It is impossible to see it [the future]. It is why I'm studies [sic]. I'm [too] old to study, I should work, but I cannot. I'm studying for the future of Myanmar. The future of Myanmar depends on the single people. (OL INT)

Many agreed that each one of them had responsibility for the future of their country and that getting rid of the military was paramount. One way to move forwards was education. The youth needed to be educated.

> There is no future for the youth, we are the only resource for Myanmar and we are not developed. As long as the military rules, there is no future. (OL INT)

Their decision to go abroad and finish their education was also framed as part of the future development of their country. '*Young people want to go abroad and it is the best thing that they can do.*'

> The future looks bad, but we are trying. Politically all young people are trying to help the country. We all want to return to Myanmar to help rebuild in education, politics, economy and environmental issues as well as human rights. We have to improve. I am confident that we will do this. (OL INT)

But at the time of the interviews, going abroad had become more difficult. The SAC had started to restrict the outflow of young people early on by making it harder to get passports. The new system requires passport applicants to apply for particular types of passports, issued only for certain purposes and which are valid for limited amounts of time. Leaving as a student was also made more difficult with the enforcement of the conscription law already mentioned. Now every township makes lists of the young people – boys and more recently girls – who might be called upon to join up, making it impossible for them to leave.[17]

> Every day is changing. Visa and passport are become [sic] a huge problem because the youth is leaving the country. Conscription law is bad for young people. I believe better days are coming after the big storm. (OL INT)

As with the students on the border, there were feelings of guilt, with one student asking:

> Young people going to other countries, only old people will be left and I worry about this. Who will take care of old people? (OL INT)

Overall, these students felt they had to go on. In some way there was no choice, as their friends had given their lives for the Revolution.

> I expect it to be better and safer for our people, especially because I have a group of people who are in jail and died. I wish my friends could get out of jail and some have to live in the border areas – I want them to come back and stay at home peacefully. (OL INT)

Conclusion and analysis

This chapter explored the diverse views and voices of young people directly engaged in the Revolution, as well as some who, though not directly engaged, have found their lives turned upside down by the coup. All have had to leave Myanmar, whether to survive, to fight, to study or to simply live. None of them chose this pathway and most have lost everything they had. Respondents, therefore, have had to rethink their lives and find agency in a new way going forward. In doing so they have not only begun to redesign their lives but also reimagine their country's future. This future Myanmar looks quite different from the kind of country emerging after the decade of reforms. As the quote – '*... the Spring Revolution is not regime change – it's a system change*' – shows, students want a break from the past and believe that the future requires a collective mindset change.

Returning to the theoretical framework, these voices reflect the youth social movement lens but also strengthen the last prism of the theoretical framework – the resistance to the neoliberal status quo. Although the students recognise the need for universities in creating an educated work force, they put the theme of 'mindset change' at the heart of the role of higher education and the new education structures they want to see in Myanmar. As Proserpio (2025) explained, the higher education the students want for themselves and for Myanmar is about learning and acquiring knowledge but is also connected with resilience and resistance. Their resistance is towards the SAC, to be sure, but it goes further, encompassing a systematic change that breaks away from the donor vision of the reform period. It is therefore fitting to call this a Revolution – a movement that strives to eradicate the old structures and rebuild the country on new values. This trajectory has revolutionary knowledge making at its heart. '*We can win. All the people who join the Revolution are trying their best*' (OL INT). May they persevere.

Notes

1 Some interviewees showed an incomplete understanding of what such ethnic and religious equality would really mean and look like. It remains to be seen if the emerging understanding of ethnic grievances will remain and transform into some form of inclusive societal governance structure. However, the shift in discourse and mindset is significant.

2 Whilst these types of attacks have ceased in Yangon, they have continued elsewhere around the country.

3 Shan State Progressive Party (Shan State Army North) – mainly operating in Northen Shan State.

4 United Wa State Army – mainly operating in North-Eastern Shan State.

5 Arakan Army – mainly operating in Rakhine State but also in Chin State.

6 Karen National Union – mainly operating in Karen State but also in Mon State and Bago Region.

7 Karenni National Progressive Party – mainly operating in Kayah State.

8 Kachin Independence Army – mainly operating in Kachin State.
9 Myanmar National Democratic Alliance Army (MNDAA), AA and TNLA.
10 At the time of writing, the Tatmadaw remain in control of the main urban areas including Yangon, Nay Pyi Taw and Mandalay.
11 In their introduction to a special issue of the *Journal of Contemporary Asia*, Chambers and Cheesman (2024) discuss how solidarity across ethnic lines is a key feature of the articles in that volume. In particular, see Cecile Medail and Saw Chit Thet Tun's contribution, which explores how Bamar elites and ordinary people have started rethinking ethnic privilege and inter-group solidarity.
12 It is also unclear how the youth located in areas controlled by the AA, MNDA, SSPP, UWSA and so on feel about the Spring Revolution.
13 The report was published in 2022 and it stated that these numbers were since February 2021.
14 (စစ်ကြောင်စီကြြိုင်တုတ် Non CDM ဝန်ထြီးြျားအား အဖပစ်ရပးအရေးယူြြည်ဟု NUG ထုတ်ဖပန်, 2022) cited in Nyan Lynn Thit Analytica (2022b), p. 3.
15 These findings are also reflected in Nyan Lynn Thit Analytica (2022b), which aimed to bring the voices of non-CDMers to the table.
16 The EMPM scholarship allows recipients to go to a participating ASEAN University (where their prior learning is credited) and finish their degree, rather than starting again from scratch. Some have had to adjust their subject of study somewhat, as host universities might not offer exactly what they started. For example, one student who had studied textile engineering is now studying environmental engineering.
17 EMPM allowed some scholarship recipients to leave early so that they would not be blocked by the conscription law being implemented.

Epilogue

> 'Unless we tell our story, then we don't exist. If you don't have somebody to talk to, if you don't have somebody listening to your story, then you effectively disappear. You become voiceless. I had the experience as a child of becoming voiceless. So I'm very much aware of people and nations who become voiceless and who are not heard. The important thing about writing and storytelling is that it allows us to exist.' – Hugo Hamilton, via The Creative Independent (LWS words of wisdom 28 February 2025)

Looking back at the genesis of this book, this quote helps explain the reason for writing it. This is obviously not about our story as authors, but the story of the students we met. Some of them told us they felt voiceless and unheard, their mission forgotten or ignored by the world in an era of poly-crisis. This book wants to make sure that they do not remain voiceless – this book is a way of helping the Spring Revolution exist. This is important not only internationally but also domestically, as a sense of 'normalisation' has taken hold of the urban centres, in particular Yangon. The tourists and most of the aid agencies are gone, but traffic still clogs the streets, young people go out partying and schools as well as universities have reopened. Children, young people and teachers put on their uniforms in the morning, catch the bus and go to study or work. There is no sense that just a couple of hours' drive outside of Yangon a fierce war is raging with Tatmadaw soldiers, PDF youths and KNU recruits killing each other. In cities like Yangon, Nay Pyi Taw and Mandalay, the Spring Revolution no longer seems to exist; it looks like the military has won. But the reality of these urban centres is not the reality of the majority of Myanmar's more than 50 million citizens.

The conflict map in Chapter 2 reflects the situation at the time of writing and shows a complex picture of resistance. The expansive edited volume by Simpson and Farrelly (2023) shows that there is a nationwide opposition movement fuelled by youth, women, ethnic nationality people and previously unrecognised minorities. Their opposition and resistance to the SAC has become creative, using decentralised governance, online and alternative education systems and digital media campaigns. They are developing many different alternative visions of a future Myanmar – federal, feminist, inclusive, plural and democratic. As the resistance has grown, so has the repression. The Assistance Association for Political Prisoners put the number of activists and civilians killed since the coup at over 5,280 (AAPP 2024). These numbers do not include all those who have died taking up arms against the dictatorship. In addition, there were over 26,000 captured and detained, of which over 20,000 remain captive.

It is important to remember that the story of resistance against the Tatmadaw is both older and broader than what has emerged since the 2021 coup, encompassing the EAO resistance that forms part of the Revolution in Chin, Kachin, Kayah and Karen States; as well as the EAO fighting that is anti-SAC but not part of the Revolution. As mentioned in Chapter 4, in Mon State things have become more complex as the NMSP – unlike its EAO neighbour the KNU – did not initially side with the Spring Revolution, and alternative armed elements emerged. The resistance in Mon is linked more closely with education than armed fighting, since the Mon National Education Committee, although part of the NMSP, is using an expansion of their education system into higher education as part of the resistance. There is also fighting that resists the Tatmadaw but is not part of the Spring Revolution, such as the conflict in Rakhine State led by the Arakan Army. The picture is complicated further by inter-EAO conflicts, such as those in Shan State. None of these facets have been dealt with in this book; these voices are almost impossible to collect.

The voices in this book reflect only one part of the resistance to the SAC that is at the core of the Revolution. The volume has focused mostly on those based on the Thai–Myanmar border, those who have made it their mission to resist the SAC with their minds, through education.[1] This book has shown that the struggle for democracy in Myanmar is not only being fought on battlefields but in classrooms and universities, both online and in the real world. Discussions with the students have provided glimpses of their vision for Myanmar. This vision, however, is not shared by all, and deep divisions have emerged between those who have supported the Revolution from the start and those who have not. What follows is a brief account, from the perspective of those who want to build a new country, of how some of these views have evolved over time and what this might mean for the future of Myanmar.

To be CDM or not to be CDM

At the time of wrapping up this volume, the evolving perspectives on the responsibilities of the CDM and of non-CDM participants in Myanmar's ongoing Revolution against the military coup reveal a complex and nuanced landscape of opinions and attitudes. The chapters of this book have shown that those who joined the Civil Disobedience Movement did so because they felt a responsibility towards the country. Those who founded the PDFs and the Spring Universities were driven by their desire to create a new Myanmar. Both the armed and the intellectual resistance movement have their role to play in this Revolution. The respondents quoted in Chapter 5 told us how they resented those who had meekly accepted the coup, who had not joined the resistance early on, who had waited to see what would happen without taking sides. Initially, there was widespread resentment towards them. Even those who joined late – either because of conscription, or because their lives had become untenable – were not seen as true resistance fighters. The book has discussed how the Revolution has taken longer than expected and how the fight has proven more challenging than anticipated. As the Revolution has progressed, attitudes have become more varied. Follow-up research conducted in February and March 2025 in Mae Sot and Chiang Rai revealed more nuanced perspectives on the division between CDM and non-CDM participants. Some CDM supporters have developed a greater understanding of the difficulties faced by non-CDM individuals, recognising the pressure they may be under and the complexity of each situation. One respondent explained this shift in attitude: '*At first, I just didn't call them. I unfriended them on Facebook. But 3–4 years after the coup d'état, my thoughts changed. I became more open-minded. I also started to think about their difficulties and their existence*' (INT CR). This quote illustrates how time and reflection have led to a more empathetic view of those who didn't join the CDM.

The implementation of conscription and increased oppression affecting all citizens have also contributed to changing perspectives. Some respondents noted that the SAC's oppression now extends to all populations, including non-CDM individuals, leading to a sense of shared suffering. As one interviewee put it, showing some empathy, '*Over time, the junta's oppression has extended to all populations including non-CDM. As we suffer during this period, the non-CDM people inside the country are also facing oppression*' (INT CR).

Many respondents now acknowledge that there are different types of non-CDM individuals and many different reasons why some might not have joined the movement. Family responsibilities, risks to livelihood and lack of political awareness were among the reasons cited. Healthcare and education were seen as necessary for the public good, leading to a more nuanced view of non-participation from actors working in these sectors. One respondent articulated this perspective, stating, '*We need to categorise the service sectors like education and healthcare that are needed for the public; they should stop the CDM. But for staff like police, army, and immigration who support the direct oppression of the junta, I disagree with them*' (INT MS). This quote highlights the recognition that certain essential services need to continue functioning for the benefit of the population at large, including the vulnerable and elderly who require medical care, and children who need basic education. Intentional support for the SAC from those who work in the wider governance structure that allows oppression was seen as different. Another respondent differentiated between basic and higher education: '*At the university level, my views haven't changed. But for basic education, I think children need schools for their personal and social development*' (INT CR).

However, it's important to note that hardline views persist among CDM supporters. These individuals maintain strong opposition to non-CDM participants – whatever their reasons might be – arguing that they enable the SAC's continued operation. One respondent explained: '*The Revolution has lasted long because of non-CDM people. [Without them] the mechanism of the military council would stop*' (INT MS). Another expressed this sentiment forcefully: '*My attitude has not changed. It was the same at the beginning ... now it's even worse ... because SAC bombed people in schools. Only non-CDM soldiers bombed people with the army*' (INT MS).

As a result of this ongoing debate, the question of how to treat non-CDM individuals after the Revolution has become a widely discussed topic. Opinions vary, ranging from calls for punishment to more nuanced approaches that consider individual circumstances and different work sectors. Some argue for a balanced approach, recognising that blanket punishment could harm the country's rebuilding efforts. As one respondent noted, '*Non-CDM like soldiers, police, and those who support the conscription law, who are related to criminal activities and the oppression of the junta, should be punished not just because of being non-CDM. Punishing non-CDM is being discussed, but if we think only in black and white, there will be many side effects*' (INT MS).

There is also recognition that the country cannot be rebuilt solely by those who supported the Revolution, as there may not be enough people or expertise. This pragmatic view echoes the approach taken during the education reforms after 2015, when the NLD took over the government. Mass sackings of bureaucrats and officials who had worked for the junta had been considered, but ultimately not implemented due to the practical realities of running public services for over 50 million people. While few people were actively part of the resistance, many disliked the junta. The same goes for today. Respondents introduced the term 'watermelon' (non-CDM who help the resistance – green outside, red inside) for those who support the Revolution but do not show their true colours. It has become clear that the sympathies of many who had not taken sides publicly lie with the Revolution, and that some were even clandestinely helping the resistance in whatever way they could. '*There are different types of non-CDMers. Some joined due to difficult situations, some are even "watermelons"*' (INT CR).

Discussions about rewarding CDM supporters have also taken place. Some suggest providing benefits such as capacity building for CDM students, better pensions for staff and consideration for promotion: '*CDMers need recognition. CDM is very difficult; they face a lot of difficulties in their daily lives, like losing their previous jobs and honour. They support the betterment of the country*' (INT MS). However, there is wariness about offering excessive benefits, with one respondent stating: '*Not excessive benefits like the military offers their groups. If there are too many opportunities, it's not good for the long term as some CDM might lack capacity*' (INT MS).

What emerges is a deep divide that presents a significant challenge for Myanmar's future. The faultline that runs across the whole of Myanmar society raises questions about reconciliation and rebuilding once the Revolution succeeds. '*The CDM movement started to end military dictatorship. But how qualified are non-CDM people? How do we measure who lost how much and who gained how much? How do we rebuild a divided society rather than just taking punitive actions? We cannot achieve democracy through bullying*' (INT CR). The range of views on this issue reflects the complexity of the situation and underscores the importance of finding a balance between accountability and the pragmatic aspects of rebuilding the country with people who might not share the revolutionary vision of the resistance. As the Revolution continues, it is also clear that perspectives on CDM and non-CDM participants are not static. They evolve with time, personal experiences and changing circumstances. The ongoing debate about how to treat non-CDM individuals after the Revolution will not go away, complicating relations between those under SAC rule and those living in liberated areas or across the border in Thailand. Nevertheless, according to Nyan Lynn Thit Analytica (2022b, p. 4), what needs to be remembered is that 'the CDM movement is the personal decision in the anti-military dictatorship, and cannot be forced by anyone.' Whether this will be taken into account when the Revolution succeeds remains to be seen.

Conscription

Conscription has also complicated things and widened the battle the resistance has to fight. Starting in April 2024, it has created a gloomy atmosphere for people living under SAC control, whether in rural areas or major cities like Yangon.[2] Not only those within the target age range (18–35 for men, 18–27 for women), but also their families (parents, spouses and children), are deeply concerned about the sudden possibility of being sent to the battlefield – township administrators and schools have been asked by the authorities to provide lists of eligible young people (The Irrawaddy 2025). This abrupt enforcement of the conscription law, enshrined in the 2008 Constitution but not used prior to the coup, is seen as a response to the Tatmadaw's significant losses on multiple frontlines.[3] Many individuals who had previously stayed out of the resistance (such as those who had not joined the CDM or the PDFs) have suddenly found themselves in a position where they can no longer avoid involvement in the ongoing armed conflict.

Following the announcement in February 2024 that approximately 5,000 people would be recruited each month, panic spread across the country. Many within the conscription age group desperately sought ways to leave Myanmar, believing that fleeing was their only means of avoiding service to the Tatmadaw. Long queues formed at embassies, and some individuals tried to secure employment abroad legally (or even illegally crossed the border) (NHK World Japan 2024; Ng 2024; Ratcliff and Soe 2024). Some ethnic minorities living in Yangon decided to return to their hometowns, fearing they would be among the first to be drafted. Since the law temporarily exempts students from conscription, some chose to enrol in SAC-run universities or other educational institutions. For CDM students this has presented a difficult dilemma, thus many sought opportunities to study abroad.

As conscription continues, the anxiety has spread further and deepened.[4] In some areas, ward or village tract administrators collect monthly fees, delaying the actual listing of those who pay. There are even reports that some individuals – likely from poor households – are being 'bought' with cash to serve as substitutes for others. Beyond the official conscription process, numerous cases have emerged of young men forcibly taken from towns or off the streets and sent to training facilities, demonstrating the SAC's urgent need to mobilise soldiers at any cost (RFA Burmese 2025c, 2025d).These incidents have instilled fear among young people, keeping them off the streets in the evening. Even in a city like Yangon, the streets are now deserted at night.

The new amendments to the conscription law, issued at the end of January 2025, are clearly aimed at strengthening the recruitment drive (Development Media Group 2025; Myanmar (CRPH) Support Group Norway 2025). Government employees are no longer exempt, and displaced persons living in other parts of the country can also be drafted. Those who are summoned are prohibited from travelling abroad without permission from the central authorities. Additionally, if a summoned individual fails to register without valid justification, their family may face punishment for their evasion of military service.[5]

In line with the new amendments to the conscription law, the SAC has also tightened regulations aimed at curbing the rapid emigration of youth since the end of January 2025. The issuance of the Overseas Worker Identification Card (OWIC), a required document for legal overseas employment, was halted in January for those within the conscription age range. Subsequently, all OWIC issuance was suspended for about a month from February to March 2025. In the middle of March 2025, a new restrictive notification was issued to further reduce the number of workers permitted to go abroad each month (Eleven Media Group 2025).

At the time of writing, students appear to remain exempt from conscription. However, the increasingly stringent regulations suggest that there is no guarantee that they will not become targets in the future. In fact, reports indicate that the listing of students at schools has already begun (The Irrawaddy 2025). It is reported that the number of young people trying to apply for passports to study abroad has been on the rise since June 2025.[6] Yet those studying abroad could also be at risk if the restrictions on overseas workers are any indication of future policies.

As armed conflicts continue to escalate across Myanmar, the need for conscripts is not confined to the Tatmadaw. In the country's long history of armed struggle, forced recruitment by EAOs has been a recurrent practice as well. For instance, in February 2024, the Restoration Council of Shan State (RCSS) announced that all residents of its controlled areas between the ages of 18 and 45 would be required to serve in the military for six years to defend the territory (The Irrawaddy 2024). Similarly, Naw Theresa (2024) reports that the Myanmar National Democratic Alliance Army (MNDAA) abducted men from refugee camps and convoys and imposed manpower quotas on local communities during its Operation 1027 offensive in northern Shan State. Comparable allegations have been made against the Ta'ang National Liberation Army (TNLA), which has developed a reputation for targeting not only its own communities but also neighbouring ethnic groups through forced recruitment. In Chin and Rakhine States, the Arakan Army (AA) has likewise reportedly compelled villagers to serve as porters and required local communities to undergo military training or provide financial contributions.

Such practices in both SAC- and non-SAC-controlled areas, have presumably disrupted the daily lives of affected communities. Families live in constant fear that their children or other household members will be taken, forcing them to hide, flee or devise costly strategies to avoid recruitment. These dynamics contribute not only to deepening poverty but also to widespread social fragmentation, as communities are torn between survival strategies and competing demands from the armed groups.

Earthquake and elections

On 28 March 2025, a powerful earthquake (magnitude 7.7) struck central Myanmar – an event of a scale not experienced in a century. The death toll has been estimated at between 3,600 and 5,350, with over 11,000 injured (Shirzaei et al. 2025). According to the United Nations Office for the Coordination of Humanitarian Affairs (OCHA 2025b), more than 17 million people across 58 townships were affected. Among them, over 9.1 million reside in the most severely impacted areas. Mandalay, Sagaing and Bago Regions accounted for more than 80 per cent of the total damage (World Bank 2025). Even prior to the earthquake, 4.3 million people in these regions were already highly vulnerable due to ongoing armed conflict (OCHA 2025a). The disaster only deepened their precarity. Strong aftershocks persisted for months, leaving affected populations in a prolonged state of insecurity.

The economic consequences of the earthquake has been equally devastating (Bissinger 2025). According to the World Bank (2025), direct economic losses are estimated at US $10.97 billion, equivalent to 14 per cent of Myanmar's GDP for fiscal year 2024/5. Widespread damage to infrastructure (including roads, bridges, dams and public buildings) has severely hampered access to clean water, healthcare and other essential services.[7] Household consumption losses among directly affected populations are estimated to range between 17 and 36 per cent, with poorer households disproportionately affected. As most affected communities depend on agriculture and casual labour for both income and subsistence, there are growing concerns about the recovery of their livelihood, with disruption to upcoming planting seasons due to limited access to seeds, fertilisers and other critical inputs (FAO and WFP 2025).

In SAC-controlled areas such as Nay Pyi Taw, the earthquake caused extensive damage to government buildings and staff accommodations, resulting in widespread administrative paralysis (International Crisis Group 2025). It is highly likely that many ministries operated in a state of near-total dysfunction in the aftermath of the quake – regardless of any intention to act – thus failing to coordinate a meaningful response.

In other contexts, such a disaster might have triggered large-scale emergency relief and rehabilitation efforts. The SAC was quick to declare a state of emergency in the worst-affected areas and to appeal for international aid (Mizzima 2025). It is highly likely that the SAC's acceptance of aid was driven by a desire for international recognition. Given the political motivations involved, the response from the international community was relatively slow in proportion to the scale of the disaster, except for countries like China, India and Thailand, which maintain relatively good relations with the SAC.[8] Moreover, the SAC was selective in determining which countries or teams were permitted to provide assistance. For example, it rejected help from Taiwanese rescue teams, likely out of deference to China (Younger 2025). Furthermore, fearing that aid shipments might contain weapons or materials intended for anti-SAC forces, the SAC blocked access roads to severely affected areas such as Sagaing (which included some of the hardest-hit locations as well as territories under the control of anti-SAC forces) and subjected humanitarian goods and services to intense scrutiny. These measures ultimately hampered the efforts of humanitarian organisations to deliver assistance (Butler 2025).

The NUG also appealed to the international community for assistance and called on donors to move away from conventional aid – delivery mechanisms. Instead, they emphasised cross-border aid delivery and sought to coordinate with various EAOs to allow humanitarian assistance to pass through their territories. In some cases, the EAOs even provided temporary shelter to those affected by the disaster (Macan-Markar 2025).

This kind of politicisation of international assistance is not new in Myanmar's context. A notable precedent is Cyclone Nargis in 2008, a catastrophic disaster that claimed over 130,000 lives and devastated the Irrawaddy Delta. In its aftermath, the international community sought to use humanitarian aid as a means to initiate political dialogue with the military regime. However, the junta initially rejected external assistance, fearing interference in their planned constitutional referendum (Selth 2008). Eventually, under mounting pressure, a compromise was reached through the formation of the Tripartite Core Group (ASEAN, the UN and the Myanmar government), which allowed for a coordinated response. The catastrophe also catalysed the emergence and expansion of grassroots civil society initiatives (Lall 2016).

In contrast, the recent earthquake saw both the SAC and NUG politicise aid, each seeking legitimacy. The concerns over the politicisation or even weaponisation of humanitarian aid are shared by all actors involved – not only the SAC, the NUG, the PDFs and the EAOs but also international donors. In this context, local and international civil society organisations attempting to support affected communities at the grassroots level remained fragmented and operated under intense pressure (Wa Lone and Shoon Naing 2025). Consequently, many affected communities and households received only limited or moderate levels of assistance (FAO and WFP 2025, p. 17). Looking ahead to the reconstruction phase, the prospects for funding remain bleak as well. According to OCHA (2025b), funding shortfalls stood at 50 per cent even 100 days after the earthquake. This is fundamentally the result of deeper, politically embedded constraints, such as mistrust among key actors, and institutional fragmentation, that continue to hinder coordinated recovery efforts (International Crisis Group 2025).

Meanwhile, armed conflict has continued across the country despite the temporary ceasefire declared by the NUG, several EAOs and the SAC in the immediate aftermath of the earthquake (International Crisis Group 2025). According to Michaels (2025), Mandalay, Magway and Sagaing regions experienced 160 armed clashes and 139 air or drone strikes in the weeks following the disaster. Offensives and counter-offensives also intensified in other regions, with some EAOs reportedly making territorial gains.

In preparation for the national elections scheduled to begin on 28 December 2025, General Min Aung Hlaing announced the dissolution of the SAC on 31 July 2025 and established a new governing body called the 'State Security and Peace Commission', of which he remains as the chairman.[9] At the same time, the nationwide state of emergency that had been in place since the coup was formally lifted – but on the very same day, it was reimposed in 63 townships across Kachin, Kayah, Kayin, Chin, Sagaing, Magway, Mandalay, Rakhine and Shan (townships largely controlled by various anti-SAC forces). In light of the planned election, the Tatmadaw is expected to intensify counter-offensives in an effort to reassert control over contested territories wherever possible.[10] While many people remain indifferent to the planned election, seeing it as nothing more than the SAC's bid for legitimacy, there are also those who hope it could help reduce the aerial bombardments or create some room for diplomatic dialogue with certain countries.[11] These perspectives reflect feelings of stalemate and frustration as socio-economic conditions continue to deteriorate alongside the spread of armed conflict over the last four years. International recognition also plays a part in the SAC's calculations on how to regain control of the country. According to the ICG, shifting global and regional politics are enabling Myanmar's military regime to strengthen its diplomatic standing despite ongoing conflict and humanitarian crisis it has created, compounded by the earthquake. With China's strategic backing, diminished Western pressure and regional fatigue, some states are preparing to normalise ties ahead of the junta's planned but non-credible elections.

This earthquake has revealed not only Myanmar's physical vulnerability but also how ongoing conflict continues to deepen the country's humanitarian crisis. More than 3.5 million people had already been internally displaced across the country due to armed violence, while over 110,000 people are reported to be newly displaced across Bago, Magwe, Sagaing, Southern Shan and Tanintharyi since late May 2025 (OCHA 2025c). The number is expected to continue rising. Recovery from the earthquake remains stalled, while ongoing armed conflict and new crises (including monsoon-related flooding and landslides) further strain an already overwhelmed and fragmented humanitarian landscape.

As noted earlier, Yangon, the former capital, as well as Taunggyi and Pin Oo Lwin (cities under SAC control), continue to function relatively normally, serving as some of the few remaining 'safe' places in the country. Comparatively well-off displaced people from conflict zones or disaster-affected areas have sought shelter in these cities.

According to some respondents, land prices and rental costs in Yangon and its suburbs have been rising due to the continuous inflow of people. Within these urban centres, it is often difficult to sense that the country is engulfed in armed conflict, particularly during the daytime, when the streets are busy with shoppers and daily activities. However, once outside the city, numerous checkpoints and gates monitoring the movement of people and goods appear along major roads, bridges and town borders.

For many, it is a painful reminder that under the current political order and ongoing armed conflicts, there is no protection either from violence or from natural disaster. Yet it also reinforces the urgency of their struggle: to build a future in which the state protects, rather than abandons, its people.

Whither the Revolution, whither Myanmar?

The progress of the Revolution in Myanmar at the time of writing, four years after its inception, is viewed with steadfast determination rather than optimism. The general consensus is that progress has been slow, with the initial momentum of the EAO-led northern offensive waning over time. When asked about their views, respondents explained that the armed resistance has yielded both positive and negative outcomes. Resistance fighters have gained resilience and experience, evolving from protests to using homemade weapons and now possessing more sophisticated arms. '*According to my sources, resistance fighters now have resilience. They started with protests, then homemade weapons, and now have arms. The 2021 movement has more potential than previous revolution movements in Myanmar like 1988*' (INT MS). Territorial control by the resistance has increased – a key difference between this fight and that of the 1980s–90s.[12] While there are now 'liberated areas' under the control of the NUG and PDFs, not only close to the borders, but also in the Bamar heartland, the junta's response to losses has been brutal. The SAC and its army remain formidable opponents. Some believe that concerns about the potential power vacuum that could result from the junta's collapse is why China and other neighbours will continue to engage with the SAC. As one respondent noted, '*The ignorance of Western countries and pressure from neighbouring countries are also slowing the resistance movement*' (INT MS). As this book has showed, the dismay felt by the students when they realised the West would not interfere on their side has morphed into disappointment and incomprehension. In their eyes, this fight for democracy is not only not supported but seems mostly forgotten by the rest of the world.

The ultimate goal of the Revolution remains unclear, with different groups within the resistance potentially having divergent visions for the future. While the common enemy has united different groups, the NUG faces criticism for being detached from reality and failing to recognise the divide between EAOs and other resistance fighters. One respondent expressed concern about the Revolution's direction: '*According to the war and control, the Revolution is succeeding, but what is our goal for the Revolution? On the other hand, many youths have made sacrifices. Whatever federal or federal democracy, politics are complicated. The vision of revolution is not clear*' (INT MS).

Sustaining the Revolution in the future presents significant challenges. Funding is a major issue, with decreased support from the diaspora and limited resources. Some suggest that the NUG should explore new avenues for generating income, such as selling resources from captured areas and creating job opportunities for people in liberated regions. '*The Revolution needs significant funding, but we don't have many resources, so campaigns aren't raising much money. Support from the diaspora has decreased. But the NUG can still communicate internationally, so they should consider how to sell resources from areas captured by resistance forces, including agricultural products, and help people from liberated areas find work in foreign countries…*' (INT MS).

The prolonged conflict has also raised concerns about personal and familial survival. Many face financial burdens and difficulties in leaving the country. Some feel the need to prioritise self-improvement before helping others, while others believe in maintaining a collective focus on the Revolution. One respondent emphasised the importance of perseverance: '*Don't just be strong yourself without helping others. Don't give up hope... You have to make yourself like a banyan tree. Don't waste your efforts. In order to succeed in the Revolution, we must try to build ourselves up and secure financial resources*' (INT MS).

As the armed conflict continues to escalate, people on both sides are facing worsening economic hardship, but also increasing pressure to be drawn into the fighting. There is a growing recognition that the struggle will last a long time. While some consider starting businesses to support themselves and the Revolution, others are committed to staying on the physical and intellectual frontlines, continuing their efforts. The need for survival is a key factor influencing individual decisions in this ongoing conflict as the youth faces a bleak and uncertain future.

Notes

1 We have tried to include some voices from the Myanmar–India border as well; however, there was no systematic fieldwork conducted there, only an exploratory trip by one of the authors.
2 The Military Service Law 2010 was enacted by the SAC in February 2024. For the full text of the law, see the following link: http://www.asianlii.org/mm/legis/laws/pmslpadcln272010638/.
3 A USIP report also claims that the Tatmadaw is smaller than many have estimated, therefore needing extra soldiers for the extended fighting across multiple fronts. See Ye Myo Hein (2023).
4 The SAC admitted that there were 'misconducts' in the recruiting procedure in March (RFA Burmese 2025e).
5 Anecdotal stories from the field suggest that they take someone else from the same household.
6 Interview by one of the authors with the organisation dispatching workers abroad in Yangon in August 2025.
7 According to the UNICEF estimate in June 2025, 52,000 homes, 2,604 schools, 789 hospitals and thousands of religious and public buildings were destroyed (UNICEF 2025).
8 China provided emergency assistance totalling US $13.9 million. India dispatched naval vessels along with an 80-member disaster response team. Rescue teams were also deployed by Russia, Thailand, Vietnam and the United Arab Emirates. Japan sent doctors through JICA. The US pledged US $9 million and the EU 13 million Euros (Su Mon Thant 2025). But these are far from sufficient.
9 Despite the change of name – to avoid confusion – this book refers to the post-coup regime with the name and acronym it chose at the time – that is, the State Administration Council (SAC).
10 https://cdn.digitalagencybangkok.com/file/client-cdn/gnlm/wp-content/uploads/2025/08/1-August-2025-gnlm.pdf
11 Based on the interviews by one of the authors in Yangon in August 2025.
12 Cheesman (2023) offers an ethnographic account of grassroots armed resistance in central Myanmar, exploring how 'the people' have re-emerged as central revolutionary agents, organising their own administration, education and defence structures in defiance of the SAC.

References

Annawitt, Philipp. 2021. 'Myanmar's junta is in a much weaker position than many realize', *Nikkei Asia*, 9 February. Accessed 27 November 2025. https://asia.nikkei.com/opinion/myanmar-s-junta-is-in-a-much-weaker-position-than-many-realize.

Assistance Association for Political Prisoners (AAPP). 2024. *Daily Briefing in Relation to the Military Coup*. Accessed 14 June 2024. https://coup.aappb.org/.

Associated Press. 2021. '5 people jump from Myanmar building to escape police; 2 die', *The Morung Express*, 11 August. Accessed 27 November 2025. https://www.morungexpress.com/5-people-jump-from-myanmar-building-to-escape-police-2-die.

Aung Ko Ko, Elizabeth L. Rhoads, Nan Tinilarwin, Win Bo Aung and Yoon Thiri Khaing. 2024. 'Beyond federalism? Inclusion, citizenship, and minorities without territory in Myanmar's Spring Revolution', *Journal of Contemporary Asia* 54 (5): 938–61. https://doi.org/10.1080/00472336.2024.2367497.

Banki, Susan. 2021. 'Myanmar's young protesters are funny, brave and media-savvy', *News and Opinion* (The University of Sydney), 19 February. Accessed 27 November 2025. https://www.sydney.edu.au/news-opinion/news/2021/02/19/myanmars-young-protestors-are-funny-brave-and-media-savvy.html.

BBC News. 2021. 'Myanmar fitness instructor accidentally captures coup unfolding'. Video, 3 February. Accessed 27 November 2025. https://www.youtube.com/watch?v=yEHiTjViicE.

Bissinger, Jared. 2025. 'Myanmar's earthquake threatens a lasting economic scar', *Fulcrum: Analysis on Southeast Asia*, 5 May. Accessed 30 August 2025. https://fulcrum.sg/myanmars-earthquake-threatens-a-lasting-economic-scar/.

Brenner, David. 2022. 'Pacification in Asia since the end of the Cold War: Illiberal peacebuilding?'. In *The Oxford Handbook of Peace History*, edited by Charles F. Howlett, Christian Philip Peterson, Deborah D. Buffton and David L. Hostetter, 354–72. Oxford: Oxford University Press.

Brenner, David. 2024. 'Misunderstanding Myanmar through the lens of democracy', *International Affairs* 100 (2): 751–69. https://doi.org/10.1093/ia/iiae015.

British Academy and École Française d'Extrême-Orient. 2015. *Language Choice in Higher Education: Challenges and opportunities. Summary of a workshop discussion organised by the British Academy and the École Française d'Extrême-Orient*. Accessed 22 March, 2025. https://www.thebritishacademy.ac.uk/documents/1066/Myanmar_Workshop_Report_English.pdf.

Burma News International. 2024. 'NUG has established nearly 6,000 schools', 15 August. Accessed 27 November 2025. https://www.bnionline.net/en/news/nug-has-established-nearly-6000-schools?utm_source=chatgpt.com.

Butler, Gavin. 2025. 'How aid becomes a weapon in Myanmar's war zone', BBC, 2 April. Accessed 27 November 2025. https://www.bbc.com/news/articles/cp8je14g2eno.

Butwell, Richard. 1972. 'Ne Win's Burma: At the end of the first decade', *Asian Survey* 12 (10): 901–12. https://doi.org/10.2307/2643067.

'Burma Academy presentation', EuroSEAS 2024 conference, 23–25 July 2024.

Chambers, Justine and Nick Cheesman. 2024. 'Introduction: Revolution and solidarity in Myanmar', *Journal of Contemporary Asia* 54 (5): 741–58. https://doi.org/10.1080/00472336.2024.2371976.

Chambers, Justine and Saw Ner Dhu Da. 2024. '"Living with" revolution: The everyday experiences of Myanmar's Generation Z revolutionaries', *Journal of Contemporary Asia* 54 (5): 781–800. https://doi.org/10.1080/00472336.2024.2359373.

Chan, Debby. 2024. *Defying Beijing: Societal resistance to the belt and road in Myanmar*. Canberra: ANU Press.

Channon, David. 2017. 'Exploring the dynamics of higher education curriculum change in Myanmar: A case study of internationalisation in an English department'. Unpublished EdD diss., UCL Institute of Education.

Cheesman, Nick. 2021. 'Revolution in Myanmar: Fighting sovereign commandment in the name of popular will', *Arena Quarterly* 8, December. Accessed 8 May, 2025. https://arena.org.au/revolution-in-myanmar/.

Cheesman, Nick. 2023. 'Where the people are: Myanmar's armed resistance and rehabilitation of "the people" as revolutionary actor', *Arena Quarterly* 14, June: 68–73. Accessed 8 May, 2025. https://arena.org.au/where-the-people-are-myanmar/.

Christian Science Monitor Editorial Board. 2021. 'Why protest signs in Myanmar are in English', *Christian Science Monitor*, 1 March. Accessed 27 November 2025. https://www.csmonitor.com/Commentary/the-monitors-view/2021/0301/Why-protest-signs-in-Myanmar-are-in-English.

Comprehensive Education Sector Review (CESR) Team. 2013. *Technical Annex on the Higher Education Subsector*. Myanmar Comprehensive Education Sector Review (CESR) Phase 1: Rapid assessment. Accessed 22 March 2025. https://www.adb.org/sites/default/files/project-documents//46369-001-tacr-04.pdf.

Connelly, Aaron and Shona Loong. 2023. 'Conflict in Myanmar and the international response'. In *Asia-Pacific Regional Security Assessment: IISS strategic dossier*. Accessed 8 May 2025. https://web-opti-qa.iiss.org/publications/strategic-dossiers/asia-pacific-regional-security-assessment-2023/aprsa-chapter-6/.

Coppel, Nicholas. 2022. 'Myanmar executions reveal regime desperation', *The Strategist* (Australian Strategic Policy Institute), 29 July. Accessed 25 March 2025. https://asialink.unimelb.edu.au/diplomacy/article/myanmar-executions-reveal-regime-desperation.

Danish Immigration Service. 2024. *Myanmar. Security situation, return and military service*. Report. Accessed 27 November 2025. https://us.dk/media/hchlihln/myanmar-security-situation-final.pdf.

Deutsche Presse Agentur. 2009. 'Aid for Myanmar's Cyclone Nargis only a fraction of aid for tsunami', 30 April. Accessed 27 November 2025. https://reliefweb.int/report/myanmar/aid-myanmars-cyclone-nargis-only-fraction-aid-tsunami.

Development Media Group. 2025. 'Junta's introduces oppressive conscription law amendments', *Burma News International*, 27 January. Accessed 27 November 2025. https://www.bnionline.net/en/news/juntas-introduces-oppressive-conscription-law-amendments.

DW News. 2021. 'Myanmar security forces launch attacks on medics'. Video, 7 July. Accessed 27 November 2025. https://www.youtube.com/watch?v=Skyv0vezrtY.

Egreteau, Renaud. 2009. 'The repression of the August 8–12 1988 (8-8-88) uprising in Burma/Myanmar', *Mass Violence & Résistance*, 25 February. Accessed 22 March 2025. https://www.sciencespo.fr/mass-violence-war-massacre-resistance/en/document/repression-august-8-12-1988-8-8-88-uprising-burmamyanmar.html.

Egreteau, Renaud. 2022a. 'Blending old and new repertoires of contention in Myanmar's anti-coup protests (2021)', *Social Movement Studies* 22 (5–6): 822–9. https://doi.org/10.1080/14742837.2022.2140650.

Egreteau, Renaud. 2022b. *Crafting Parliament in Myanmar's Disciplined Democracy (2011–2021)*. Oxford: Oxford University Press.

Ei Khine, Mya Mya San and Coeli Barry. 2024. 'Living the Civil Disobedience Movement: An examination of the motivations and consequences for Myanmar's university teachers', *Conflict and Peace Studies Journal* 3 (2): 27–54.

Eleven Media Group. 2025. 'Ministry of Labour limits monthly job submissions to 50 for Thailand, 15 for Japan', 23 March. Accessed 27 November 2025. https://elevenmyanmar.com/news/ministry-of-labour-limits-monthly-job-submissions-to-50-for-thailand-15-for-japan.

Esson, James and Kevin Wang. 2018. 'Reforming a university during political transformation: A case study of Yangon University in Myanmar'. *Studies in Higher Education* 43 (7): 1184–95. https://doi.org/10.1080/03075079.2016.1239250.

European Commission (n.d.). 'Myanmar/Burma'. Accessed 27 November 2025. https://civil-protection-humanitarian-aid.ec.europa.eu/where/asia-and-pacific/myanmarburma_en.

FAO and WFP. 2025. *Myanmar: Post-earthquake rapid needs assessment – DIEM-Impact report, April 2025*. Rome: FAO and WFP. https://doi.org/10.4060/cd5778en.

Fauldner, Dominic. 2024. 'Myanmar military's bombing of civilians set for record year', *Nikkei Asia*, 8 July. Accessed 27 November 2025. https://asia.nikkei.com/spotlight/myanmar-crisis/myanmar-military-s-bombing-of-civilians-set-for-record-year.

Frontier Myanmar. 2023. 'To punish or pardon? CDM policy stirs debate', 6 March. Accessed 27 November 2025. https://www.frontiermyanmar.net/en/to-punish-or-pardon-cdm-policy-stirs-debate/.

Fujita, Koichi, Endo Tamaki, Okamoto Ikuko, Nakanishi Yoshihiro and Yamada Miwa. 2010. 'Myanmar migrant laborers in Ranong, Thailand', IDE Discussion Paper No. 257. Accessed 15 December 2025. https://www.ide.go.jp/English/Publish/Reports/Dp/257.html.

Fumagalli, Matteo. 2022. 'The next swing of the pendulum? Cross-border aid and shifting aid paradigms in post-coup Myanmar', *European University Institute Robert Schuman Centre Policy Papers* 8 (2022). Accessed 25 March 2025. https://cadmus.eui.eu/handle/1814/74769.

Global Education Cluster and Child Protection AoR. 2022. *Education in Emergency and Child Protection Joint Needs Assessment: Myanmar*. Accessed 27 November 2025. https://cpaor.net/sites/default/files/2023-08/Executive%20Summary_Myanmar%20Child%20Protection-Education%20Needs%20Assessment%20ENG.pdf.

Hamilton, H. (2025, 22 January). 'Writer Hugo Hamilton on telling stories for the voiceless', The Creative Independent. Accessed 27 November 2025. https://thecreativeindependent.com/people/writer-hugo-hamilton-on-telling-stories-for-the-voiceless/.

Head, Jonathan. 2023. 'Myanmar: Air strikes have become a deadly new tactic in the civil war', BBC, 31 January. Accessed 27 November 2025. https://www.bbc.com/news/world-asia-64397397.

Hedström, Jenny, Elisabeth Olivius and Kay Soe. 2023. 'Women in Myanmar: Change and continuity'. In *Myanmar: Politics, economy and society*, edited by Adam Simpson and Nicholas Farrelly, 220–36. London: Routledge.

Henschke, Rebecca, Ko Ko Aung, Jack Aung and Data Journalism Team. 2024. 'Soldier-spies in Myanmar help pro-democracy rebels make crucial gains', BBC, 20 December. Accessed 27 November 2025. https://www.bbc.com/news/articles/c390ndrny17o.

Heslop, Lynne. 2019. 'Encountering internationalisation: Higher education and social justice in Myanmar'. PhD diss., University of Sussex.

Houtman, Gustaaf. 1999. *Mental Culture in Burmese Crisis Politics: Aung San Suu Kyi and the National League for Democracy*. Institute for the Study of Languages and Cultures of Asia and Africa, Tokyo University of Foreign Studies. Accessed 27 November 2025. http:// www.burmalibrary.org/docs19/Houtman-1999-Mental_Culture_in_Burmese_Crisis_Politics.pdf.

Htet Lynn Oo. 2023. *Dynamics of 21st-Century Anti-Coup Resistance in Myanmar: Triangle Model of Resistance*. New Voices in Cultural Relations. London: British Council & BISA.

Htet Htet Eindra Aung. 2024. 'Interview: "After three years … it is impossible for these dictators to win"', *Radio Free Asia*, 1 February. Accessed 27 November 2025. https://www.rfa.org/english/news/myanmar/tayzar-san-interview-02012024161237.html.

Institute of South Asian Studies. 2021. *The Myanmar Coup, Resistance and India's Response: Fractured between words and deeds*. Special Report Issue No. 14. Singapore: National University of Singapore. Accessed 8 May 2025. https://www.isas.nus.edu.sg/wp-content/uploads/2021/06/Myanmar-Special-Report-Full.pdf.

International Cooperation Bureau, Ministry of Foreign Affairs of Japan. 2023. Official Development Assistance (ODA) Country Data. Accessed 15 December 2025. https://www.mofa.go.jp/mofaj/gaiko/oda/files/100730081.pdf#page=28.

International Crisis Group. 2021a. 'Taking aim at the Tatmadaw: The new armed resistance to Myanmar's coup', Crisis Group Asia Briefing No. 168, 28 June. Accessed 8 May 2025. https://www.crisisgroup.org/brf/asia-pacific/myanmar/b168-taking-aim-tatmadaw-new-armed-resistance-myanmars-coup.

International Crisis Group. 2021b. 'Responding to the Myanmar Coup', Crisis Group Asia Briefing No. 166 Yangon/Bangkok/Brussels, 16 February 2021. Accessed 27 November 2025. https://www.crisisgroup.org/asia-pacific/myanmar/b166-responding-myanmar-coup.

International Crisis Group. 2024a. 'Ethnic autonomy and its consequences in post-coup Myanmar', Crisis Group Asia Briefing No. 180, 30 May. Accessed 27 November 2025. http://www.jstor.org/stable/resrep60218.

International Crisis Group. 2024b. 'Scam centres and ceasefires: China–Myanmar ties since the coup', Crisis Group Asia Briefing No. 179, 27 March. Accessed 27 November 2025. https://icg-prod.s3.amazonaws.com/s3fs-public/2024-03/b179-china-myanmar.pdf.

International Crisis Group. 2025. 'Myanmar's dangerous drift: Conflict, elections and looming regional détente', Crisis Group Asia Briefing No. 184, 18 July. Accessed 27 November 2025. https://www.crisisgroup.org/brf/asia/south-east-asia/myanmar/b184-myanmars-dangerous-drift-conflict-elections-and-looming-regional-detente.

International Institute for Strategic Studies (n.d.). Myanmar Conflict Map. Accessed 27 November 2025. https://myanmar.iiss.org/.

The Irrawaddy. 2024. 'Conscription law will drive Myanmar deeper into war, ethnic armed group warns', 20 February. Accessed 27 November 2025. https://www.irrawaddy.com/news/politics/conscription-law-will-drive-myanmar-deeper-into-war-ethnic-armed-group-warns.html.

The Irrawaddy. 2025. 'Conscript-hungry Myanmar junta turns sights on students', 10 January. Accessed 27 November 2025. https://www.irrawaddy.com/news/burma/conscript-hungry-myanmar-junta-turns-sights-on-students.html?utm_source=chatgpt.com.

Jirattikorn, Amporn. 2023. 'Forced into exile: The untold journeys of Myanmar's CDM teachers', *Anthropology Today* 39 (1): 23–7. https://doi.org/10.1111/1467-8322.12791.

Jordt, Ingrid. 2021. 'Notes on the coup in Myanmar: Karmic kingship, legitimacy, and sovereignty', *Contending Modernities*, 6 April. Accessed 27 November 2025. https://workersbushtelegraph.com.au/2021/04/14/notes-on-the-coup-in-myanmar-karmic-kingship-legitimacy-and-sovereignty/.

Jordt, Ingrid, Tharaphi Than and Sue Ye Lin. 2021. 'How Generation Z galvanized a revolutionary movement against Myanmar's 2021 military coup'. Introduction. In *How Generation Z Galvanized a Revolutionary Movement against Myanmar's 2021 Military Coup*, vii–viii. Singapore: ISEAS–Yusof Ishak Institute.

Kamibeppu, Takao and Roger Y. Chao. 2017. 'Higher education and Myanmar's economic and democratic development', *International Higher Education* 88: 19–20. https://doi.org/10.6017/ihe.2017.88.9688.

Kandiko Howson, Camille and Marie Lall. 2019. 'Higher education reform in Myanmar: Neoliberalism versus an inclusive developmental agenda', *Globalisation, Societies and Education* 18 (2): 109–24. https://doi.org/10.1080/14767724.2019.1689488.

Khaing Phyu Htut, Marie Lall and Camille Kandiko Howson. 2022. 'Caught between COVID-19, coup and conflict – What future for Myanmar higher education reforms?', *Education Sciences* 12 (2): 67. https://doi.org/10.3390/educsci12020067.

Khin Khin Mra and Jenny Hedström. 2024. '"This bra protects me better than the military": Bodies and protests in the Myanmar Spring Revolution', *Journal of Contemporary Asia* 54 (5): 759–80. https://doi.org/10.1080/00472336.2024.2344117.

Khin Oo Thazin. 2021. 'Keeping the streets: Myanmar's Civil Disobedience Movement as public pedagogy', *PR&TA Journal* 1 (1). Accessed 29 November 2025. https://www.pratajournal.com/keeping-the-streets-myanmars-civil-disobedience-movement-as-public-pedagogy.

Kudo, Toshihiro. 2008. 'Myanmar's economic relations with China: Who benefits and who pays?'. In *Dictatorship, Disorder and Decline in Myanmar*, edited by Monique Skidmore and Trevor Wilson, 87–110. Canberra: ANU Press. https://press-files.anu.edu.au/downloads/press/p102401/html/ch06.html.

Kudo, Toshihiro. 2024. 'Japan's official development assistance to Myanmar: Logic of expansion and freezing'. In *ASEAN and Japan: Ever-Changing Economic Relationships*, edited by Miki Hamada, 271–305. Chiba: IDE-Japan. Accessed 25 March 2025. https://www.ide.go.jp/English/Publish/Books/Jpn_eBooks/eBook/202403_02.html.

Kuhakan, Jiraporn. 2021. 'Myanmar protesters string up women's clothes for protection', Reuters, 6 March. Accessed 27 November 2025. https://www.reuters.com/world/asia-pacific/myanmar-protesters-string-up-womens-clothes-protection-2021-03-06/.

Kyaw Ye Lynn. 2021. '5 arrested as 1st anti-coup protest staged in Myanmar', *AA*, 4 February, Accessed 27 November 2025. https://www.aa.com.tr/en/asia-pacific/5-arrested-as-1st-anti-coup-protest-staged-in-myanmar/2133534.

Kyaw Yin Hlaing. 2007. 'The politics of state–society relations in Burma', *Southeast Asia Research* 15 (2): 213–54. https://doi.org/10.5367/000000007781509571.

Kyed, Helene Maria (ed.). 2020. *Everyday Justice in Myanmar: Informal resolutions and state evasion in a time of contested transition*. Nordic Institute of Asian Studies Studies in Asian topics No. 71. Copenhagen: NIAS Press.

Lall, Marie, Thei Su San, Nwe Nwe San, Ye Htut Naing, Theint Theint Myat, Lwin Thet Thet Khaing, Swann Lynn Htet and Yin Nyein Aye. 2014. *Citizenship in Myanmar – Contemporary debates and challenges in light of the reform process*. Yangon and Bangkok: Myanmar Egress and FNS.

Lall, Marie. 2016. *Understanding Reform in Myanmar: People and society in the wake of military rule*. London: Hurst Publishers.

Lall, Marie. 2021a. *Myanmar's Education Reforms: A pathway to social justice?*. London: UCL Press. https://doi.org/10.14324/111.9781787353695.

Lall, Marie. 2021b. 'The tragedy of Myanmar higher education under the coup', *International Higher Education* 107: 37–9. https://ejournals.bc.edu/index.php/ihe/article/view/14585.

Lall, Marie and Ashley South. 2018. 'Power dynamics of language and education policy in Myanmar's contested transition', *Comparative Education Review*, 62 (4): 482–502. https://www.journals.uchicago.edu/doi/10.1086/699655.

Lall, Marie, Ashley South, Emily Stenning and Tim Schroeder with Aye Aye Tun, Nicola Edwards, Kim Jolliffe, Axel Schroeder, Viren Lall, Mi Kun Chan Non, Aung Htun, Nangzing Lu Awn and Cin Khan Lian. 2020. 'From conflict towards partnership in education – The Myanmar Education Partnership Project', policy note, Yangon: World Bank.

Lall, Marie, Camille Kandiko Howson and Aye Aye Tun. 2023. 'Higher education in Myanmar'. In *The Oxford Handbook on Higher Education in Asia*, edited by Devesh Kapur, Lily Kong, Florence Lo and David M. Malone, 837–55. Oxford: Oxford University Press.

Lall, Marie, Min Aung Mann and L. Proserpio. 2025. 'Emerging from adversity: Spring Universities in post-coup Myanmar', *Education and Conflict Review*, 5: 89–96. https://doi.org/10.14324/000.ch.10207908.

Linn, Soe Nandar. 2024. 'Myanmar faces manifold crises as military conscription drives mass exodus', *East Asia Forum*, 26 October. Accessed 27 November 2025. https://eastasiaforum.org/2024/10/26/myanmar-faces-manifold-crises-as-military-conscription-drives-mass-exodus/.

Lintner, Bertil. 1990. *Outrage: Burma's struggle for democracy*. London and Bangkok: White Lotus.

Loong, Shona. 2022. 'Post-coup Myanmar in six warscapes', The International Institute for Strategic Studies, 10 June. Accessed 27 November 2025. https://myanmar.iiss.org/analysis/introduction.

Lorch, Jasmin. 2007. 'Myanmar's civil society – a patch for the national education system?', *Südostasien Aktuell: Journal of Current Southeast Asian Affairs* 26 (3): 54–88. Accessed 27 November 2025. https://nbn-resolving.org/urn:nbn:de:0168-ssoar-336394.

Lovett, Lorcan. 2025. 'The Chin split: A simple guide', *On Myanmar*, 17 February. Accessed 27 November 2025. https://lorcanlovett.substack.com/p/the-chin-split-a-simple-guide.

Macan-Markar, Marwaan. 2025. 'Myanmar opposition calls for earthquake aid to bypass military regime', *Nikkei Asia*, 1 April. Accessed 27 November 2025. https://asia.nikkei.com/spotlight/myanmar-crisis/myanmar-opposition-calls-for-earthquake-aid-to-bypass-military-regime.

Marlar, Elena and Justine Chambers. 2023. 'Our htamein, our flag, our victory: The role of young women in Myanmar's Spring Revolution', *Journal of Burma Studies* 27 (1): 65–99. https://dx.doi.org/10.1353/jbs.2023.0002.

Matelski, Maaike. 2016. 'Civil society, foreign aid, and donor dependency in transitional Myanmar'. In *Border Twists and Burma Trajectories: Perceptions, reforms, and adaptations*, edited by Samak Kosem, 93–126. Chiang Mai: Center for ASEAN Studies, Chiang Mai University.

Medail, Cecile and Saw Chit Thet Tun. 2024. 'Instrumentalism or commitment to social justice? Shifting inter-ethnic solidarities in post-coup Myanmar', *Journal of Contemporary Asia* 54 (5): 913–37. https://doi.org/10.1080/00472336.2024.2370817.

Metro, Rosalie. 2016. 'Students and teachers as agents of democratization and national reconciliation in Burma: Realities and possibilities'. In *Metamorphosis: Studies in Social and Political Change in Myanmar*, edited by Renaud Egreteau and François Robinne, 209–33. Singapore: NUS Press. https://doi.org/10.2307/j.ctv1ntgbt.15.

Metro, Rosalie. 2017. 'Whose democracy?: The university student protests in Burma/Myanmar 2014–2016'. In *Universities and Conflict: The role of higher education in peacebuilding and conflict*, edited by Juliet Millican. London and New York: Routledge.

Michaels, Morgan. 2025. 'Assessing post-earthquake patterns of violence in Myanmar', Myanmar Conflict Update, IISS Myanmar Conflict Map. https://myanmar.iiss.org/updates/2025-05.

MIMU. 2018. 'Vulnerability in Myanmar: A secondary data review of needs, coverage and gaps'. Accessed 29 November 2025. https://themimu.info/sites/themimu.info/files/documents/Report_Vulnerability_in_Myanmar_HARP-MIMU_Jun2018_ENG_Online_version_low-res_0.pdf.

Min Zaw Oo and Stein Tønnesson. 2023. *Counting Myanmar's Dead: Reported civilian casualties since the 2021 military coup*. Peace Research Institute Oslo. Accessed 25 March 2025. https://www.prio.org/publications/13516.

Ministry of Education. 2016. *National Education Strategic Plan 2016–21*. Accessed 22 March 2025. https://www.britishcouncil.org/sites/default/files/myanmar_national_education_strategic_plan_2016-21.pdf.

Ministry of Education. 2019. *Myanmar National Educational Strategic Plan 2016–2021: Data gap analysis report*. Ministry of Education and UNESCO.

Ministry of Education. 2020a. *Mid Term Review NESP 2016–2021 Final Report*. Nay Pyi Taw: Ministry of Education. Accessed 27 November 2025. https://www.moe.gov.mm/sites/default/files/MTR_NESP_ENG.pdf.

Ministry of Education. 2020b. Myanmar COVID-19 National Response and Recovery Plan for the Education Sector. Accessed 20 March 2026. https://www.moe.gov.mm/sites/default/files/MOE_COVID19_Response_and_Recovery_Plan_03062020.pdf.

Ministry of Education, National Unity Government. 2025. NUG Education Strategy and Policy (unpublished document).

Mizzima. 2025. 'Myanmar junta asks for international aid after earthquake', 28 March. Accessed 27 November 2025. https://eng.mizzima.com/2025/03/28/20560.

Myanmar (CRPH) Support Group Norway. 2025. 'Myanmar enacts People's Military Service bylaw: travel abroad restricted without central permission for civil service designees'. Accessed 19 March 2026. https://www.crphsupportgroup.no/post/myanmar-enacts-people-s-military-service-bylaw-travel-abroad-restricted-without-central-permission.

Myanmar News Agency. 2024. 'NUG-linked university issues fake degrees for Thai university admission', *The Global: New Light of Myanmar*, 23 November. Accessed 29 November 2025. https://www.gnlm.com.mm/nug-linked-university-issues-fake-degrees-for-thai-university-admission/.

Myanmar Now. 2021. 'Junta reportedly eyeing November reopening of schools'. Accessed 20 March 2025. https://myanmar-now.org/en/news/junta-reportedly-eyeing-november-reopening-of-schools/.

Myanmar Now. 2025. 'Rival Chin groups agree to form unified "Chin National Council" after years of tension', 28 February. Accessed 29 November 2025. https://myanmar-now.org/en/news/rival-chin-groups-agree-to-form-unified-chin-national-council-after-years-of-tension/?tztc=1.

Myat Thein. 2004. *Economic Development of Myanmar*. Singapore: Institute of Southeast Asian Studies.

Nachemson, Andrew. 2021. 'In Myanmar, protesters urge police to join democracy fight', Aljazeera, 8 February. Accessed 29 November 2025. https://www.aljazeera.com/news/2021/2/8/in-myanmar-protesters-urge-police-to-join-democracy-fight.

Nai Aue Mon and Maggi Quadrini. 2024. 'Military conscription in southeastern Myanmar demands international intervention', *The Diplomat*, 7 May. Accessed 27 November 2025. https://thediplomat.com/2024/05/military-conscription-in-southeastern-myanmar-demands-international-intervention/#:~:text=Under%20the%20law%2C%20all%20men,uncertain%20amid%20the%20ongoing%20conflict.

Narai, Robert. 2022. '"Until the end of the world": Myanmar's unfinished revolution', *Marxist Left Review* 23 (Summer): 73–113. Accessed 8 May 2025. https://marxistleftreview.org/articles/until-the-end-of-the-world-myanmars-unfinished-revolution/.

Naw Say Phaw Waa. 2021. 'Students take a leading role in protests against the coup', *University World News*, 12 February. Accessed 29 November 2025. https://www.universityworldnews.com/post.php?story=20210212142743135.

Naw Theresa. 2024. 'Myanmar ethnic armed groups draw allegations of forced recruitment', *The Diplomat*, 3 January. Accessed 29 November 2025. https://thediplomat.com/2024/01/myanmar-ethnic-armed-groups-draw-allegations-of-forced-recruitment/.

Ng, Kelly. 2024. 'Myanmar: Young people attempt to flee ahead of conscription order', BBC, 26 February. Accessed 29 November 2025. https://www.bbc.com/news/world-asia-68345291.

NHK World Japan. 2024. 'Myanmar's military draft spurs exodus', 11 July. Accessed 29 November 2025. https://www3.nhk.or.jp/nhkworld/en/news/backstories/3444/.

Nora. 2023. 'We are developing the ability to make changes and build the future', *The Irrawaddy*, 23 February. Accessed 29 November 2025. https://www.irrawaddy.com/news/burma/we-are-developing-the-ability-to-make-changes-and-build-the-future.html.

Novelli, Mario, Birgül Kutan, Patrick Kane, Adnan Celik, Tejendra Pherali and Saranel Benjamin. 2024. *Laboratories of Learning. Social movements, education and knowledge-making in the Global South*. London: Pluto Press.

Nyan Lynn Thit Analytica. 2022a. *Revealing the Voices of Civil Disobedience Movement*. 28 November. Accessed 29 November 2025. https://progressivevoicemyanmar.org/2022/11/28/revealing-the-voices-of-civil-disobedience-movement/.

Nyan Lynn Thit Analytica. 2022b. *Inspecting the Actions of Mainstream Coalition toward Civil Disobedience Movement*. 18 January 2023. Accessed 29 November 2025. https://progressive voicemyanmar.org/2023/01/18/ultranationalism-militarys-attempts-to-the-state-control-2/.

Nyein Chan May. 2023. 'Myanmar: Feminismus in einem intersektionalen Widerstand?'. Stiftung Asienhaus. Accessed 24 December 2025. https://fid4sa-repository.ub.uni-heidelberg.de/4634/1/Blickwechsel_Myanmar-Feminismus.pdf.

OCHA. 2023. *Online Scam Operations and Trafficking into Forced Criminality in Southeast Asia: Recommendations for a human rights response*. Accessed 29 November 2025. https://digital library.un.org/record/4020504?v=pdf.

OCHA. 2025a. 'Myanmar earthquake humanitarian snapshot', 7 April. Accessed 29 November 2025. https://myanmar.un.org/en/292288-ocha-myanmar-earthquake-humanitarian-snapshot.

OCHA. 2025b. 'Myanmar earthquake 100 days after', 7 July. Accessed 29 November 2025. https://myanmar.un.org/en/297541-myanmar-earthquake100-days-after.

OCHA. 2025c. 'Myanmar humanitarian update No. 47,' 27 June. Accessed 29 November 2025. https://myanmar.un.org/en/297049-myanmar-humanitarian-update-no-47.

O'Connor, James. 2011. *State Building, Infrastructure Development and Chinese Energy Projects in Myanmar*. IRASEC. Accessed 25 March 2025. https://www.irasec.com/IMG/UserFiles/Files/04_Publications/Notes/State_Building-Infrastructure_Development_and_Chinese_Energy_Projects_in_Myanmar.pdf.

Okamoto, Ikuko. 2020. 'Myanmar's rural economy at a crossroads', In *Living with Myanmar*, edited by Justine Chambers, Charlotte Galloway and Jonathan Liljeblad, 157–82. Singapore: ISEAS–Yusof Ishak Institute.

Pedersen, Morten B. 2023. 'Democracy and human rights under military rule'. In *Myanmar: Politics, economy and society*, edited by Adam Simpson and Nicholas Farrelly, 75–90. London: Routledge.

PIME Asia News. 2006. 'Constitution deliberations resume as student protests grow', 11 October. Accessed 29 November 2025. https://www.asianews.it/news-en/Constitution-deliberations-resume-as-student-protests-grow-7446.html.

Prasse-Freeman, Elliott. 2023. *Rights Refused: Grassroots activism and state violence in Myanmar*. Stanford, CA: Stanford University Press.

Prasse-Freeman, Elliott and Tani Sebro. 2021. 'The view of the coup from the camp: Myanmar's emergent trans-ethnic solidarity', *The Georgetown Journal of International Affairs*, 17 March. Accessed 29 November 2025. https://gjia.georgetown.edu/2021/03/17/https-twitter-com-natrani-status-1360993418445524999-photo-1/.

Prasse-Freeman, Elliott and Ko Kabya. 2021. 'Revolutionary responses to the Myanmar coup', *Anthropology Today* 37 (3): 1–2. https://doi.org/10.1111/1467-8322.12649.

Proserpio, Licia. 2025. *Resistance through Higher Education: Myanmar universities' struggle against authoritarianism*, 1st edition. Bristol: Bristol University Press. https://doi.org/10.2307/jj.12348206.

Proserpio, Licia and Antonio Fiori. 2022. 'Myanmar universities in the post-coup era: The clash between old and new visions of higher education', TWAI, 1 December. Accessed 18 March 2025. https://www.twai.it/articles/myanmar-universities-post-coup-era/.

Rahmat, Rozi Binte, Tom Porta and Kay Thwe Phyo. 2025. 'The role of the higher education educator in times of conflict in Myanmar', *Teaching in Higher Education* 31 (1): 1–19. https://doi.org/10.1080/13562517.2025.2512334.

Ratcliffe, Rebecca and Aung Naing Soe. 2024. '"They have lists of everyone's names": Myanmar conscription law unleashes wave of fear', *The Guardian*, 28 February. Accessed 29 November 2025. https://www.theguardian.com/global-development/2024/feb/28/myanmar-military-conscription-law-details.

Regan, Helen, Sandi Sidhu and Clarissa Ward. 2021. '"I thought I would die". Myanmar protesters describe torture they suffered in detention', CNN, 27 April. Accessed 29 November 2025. https://edition.cnn.com/2021/04/27/asia/myanmar-coup-detainees-torture-intl-hnk/index.html.

RFA Burmese. 2025a. 'Students from coup-hit Myanmar lament loss of canceled "DEI" scholarships', *Radio Free Asia*, 3 February. Accessed 29 November 2025. https://www.rfa.org/english/myanmar/2025/02/03/myanmar-dei-scholarships-canceled/.

RFA Burmese. 2025b. 'Military council arrests seven people involved in notarizing NUG-issued diplomas', *Radio Free Asia*, 10 March. Accessed 29 November 2025. https://www.rfa.org/burmese/news/military-arrrest-nug-degree-certificate-notry-03102025130210.html.

RFA Burmese 2025c. '"Snatch and recruit" arrests in Myanmar target youth for military service', *Radio Free Asia*, 2 January. Accessed 29 November 2025. https://www.rfa.org/english/myanmar/2025/01/02/myanmar-snatch-recruit-conscription/.

RFA Burmese. 2025d. 'Junta troops forcibly recruit more than 70 young men in Myanmar town', *Radio Free Asia*, 17 March. Accessed 29 November 2025. https://www.rfa.org/english/myanmar/2025/03/17/myanmar-70-men-arrested-for-conscription/.

RFA Burmese. 2025e. 'Myanmar junta admits misconduct in its controversial conscription scheme', *Radio Free Asia*, 21 March. Accessed 29 November 2025. https://www.rfa.org/english/myanmar/2025/03/21/myanmar-junta-recruitment-misconduct-admit/.

Rieffel, Lex and James W. Fox. 2013. 'Too much, too soon? The dilemma of foreign aid to Myanmar/Burma', *The Brookings Institute*, 15 March. Accessed 25 March 2025. https://www.brookings.edu/wp-content/uploads/2016/06/03-foreign-aid-myanmar-burma-rieffel-fox-2.pdf.

Rinehart, Gray, Tejendra Pherali, Elaine Chase, Htet Thiha Zaw and Thein Naing. 2024. 'Diversity and fragmentation of Myanmar education: Schooling shaped by protracted conflict and crisis', ERICC Working Paper. New York: IRC.

Rives, Nang Mo Lao. 2014. 'University student activism in Burma/Myanmar during the 1980s'. PhD diss., University of Kansas. https://eric.ed.gov/?id=ED580529.

Rizky, Bima Nur Muhammad. 2021. 'The path to democracy? Foreign aid post-military coup in Myanmar', *Global Focus* 1 (2): 150–63. https://doi.org/10.21776/ub.jgf.2021.001.02.4.

Ryan, Megan, Mai Van Tran and Swan Ye Htut. 2024. 'Strange bedfellows or trusted comrades? Digital solidarity building among Myanmar's revolutionaries', *Journal of Contemporary Asia* 54 (5): 887–912. https://doi.org/10.1080/00472336.2024.2330933.

Sarma, J. and Kapur, R. 2021. *The Myanmar Coup, Resistance and India's Response: Fractured between words and deeds. Special Report No. 14.* Institute of South Asian Studies, National University of Singapore. Accessed 8 May 2025. https://www.isas.nus.edu.sg/wp-content/uploads/2021/06/Myanmar-Special-Report-Full.pdf.

Selth, Andrew. 2008. 'Burma and the threat of invasion: Regime fantasy or strategic reality', Griffith University Regional Outlook Paper No. 17. Accessed 29 November 2025. https://www.griffith.edu.au/__data/assets/pdf_file/0025/1371049/Andrew-Selth-Regional-Outlook-17v2.pdf.

Shirzaei, Manoochehr, Shubham Awasthi, Esther O. Oyedele, Mohammad Khorrami, Nivedita Kamaraj, Susanna Werth, Mir Matin andKaveh Madani. 2025. *Building Damage Assessment of the March 2025 Myanmar Earthquake*. Richmond Hill, ON: United Nations University Institute for Water, Environment and Health (UNU-INWEH). https://doi.org/10.53328/INR24MSIR002.

Simpson, Adam and Nicholas Farrelly. 2021. 'As killings, beatings and disappearances escalate, what's the end game in Myanmar?', *The Conversation*, 10 March. Accessed 29 November 2025. https://theconversation.com/as-killings-beatings-and-disappearances-escalate-whats-the-end-game-in-myanmar-156752.

Simpson, Adam and Nicholas Farrelly (eds.). 2023. *Myanmar: Politics, Economy and Society*, 2nd edition. London: Routledge.

Slow, Oliver. 2023. 'The mobile game funding a revolution in Myanmar', BBC, 27 August. Accessed 29 November 2025. https://www.bbc.com/news/world-asia-65906961.

Soe San. 2021, 17 May. 'Beyond the coup in Myanmar: Don't let the light of education be extinguished'. *Beyond the Myanmar Coup*. Just Security/Human Rights Clinic, Harvard Law School. Accessed 29 November 2025. https://humanrightsclinic.law.harvard.edu/beyond-the-coup-in-myanmar-dont-let-the-light-of-education-be-extinguished/.

South, Ashley, Jasminpaw, Jacqueline Hpway, Angela Aung, Eileen May, Mi Kun Chan Non and Anne-Meike Fechter. 2023. 'Protracted displacement, local economies and protection: Communities and ethnic armed organisations in Myanmar', *Humanitarian Practice Network* 82, 10 January. Accessed 8 May 2025. https://odihpn.org/publication/protracted-displacement-local-economies-and-protection-communities-and-ethnic-armed-organisations-in-myanmar/.

South, Ashley, Susanne Kempel, Malin Perhult and Nils Carstensen. 2011. *Myanmar – surviving the storm: Self-protection and survival in the Delta*. Local to Global Protection (L2GP). Accessed 29 November 2025. https://www.local2global.info/wp-content/uploads/L2GP_Myanmar_Nargis_study.pdf.

South, Ashley, Emily Stenning and Tim Schroeder. 2024. 'Education reform in post-coup Myanmar: Federalizing or federating?', *Contemporary Southeast Asia* 46 (2): 318–41. Accessed 8 May 2025. https://www.jstor.org/stable/27422395.

Spring University Myanmar. 2023. *Higher Education in Post-coup Myanmar*. Accessed 25 March 2025. https://www.springuniversitymm.com/_files/ugd/1c2e5f_a30dd3d3ff7f48f8837170 11848e4864.pdf.

Su Mon Thant. 2025. 'Myanmar earthquake: Why the junta has turned away aid', *The Interpreter*, 2 May. Accessed 29 November 2025. https://www.lowyinstitute.org/the-interpreter/ myanmar-earthquake-why-junta-has-turned-away-aid.

Symaco, Lorraine Pe and Martin Hayden, eds. 2024. *The International Handbook on Education in Southeast Asia*. Singapore: Springer Nature. https://doi.org/10.1007/978-981-16-8136-3.

Tanaka, T. (pseud.). 2023. 'Humanitarian and beyond: Assistance led by Myanmar citizens in the Thai border areas and its implications for the regional response to Myanmar's post-coup crisis', Policy Paper, University of London.

Thant Myint-U. 2001. *The Making of Modern Burma*. Cambridge: Cambridge University Press.

Thawnghmung, Ardeth Maung and Gwen Robinson. 2025. 'Myanmar's uncharted territories: Pitfalls and prospects in emergent forms of governance', *Trends in Southeast Asia, No. 16*. Singapore: ISEAS–Yusof Ishak Institute. Accessed 18 March 2026. https://www.cambridge. org/core/books/abs/myanmars-uncharted-territories/myanmars-uncharted-territories-pitfa lls-and-prospects-in-emergent-forms-of-governance/D14CB5E6DF5BE3020E4F7F2D4DB57 963#chapter.

Thein-Lemelson, Seinenu M. 2021. '"Politicide" and the Myanmar coup', *Anthropology Today* 37 (2): 3–5. https://doi.org/10.1111/1467-8322.12639.

Tin Maung Htwe. 2023. 'Dynamics of struggle and collaboration: Student and youth activism in Myanmar's 2021 Spring Revolution'. In *Resist! Democracy and Youth Activism in Myanmar, Hong Kong, and Singapore*, edited by Amy Freedman and Joseph Tse-Hei Le, 44–66. New York: Pace University Press.

Tonkin, Derek. 2007. 'The 1990 elections in Myanmar: Broken promises or a failure of communication?', *Contemporary Southeast Asia* 29 (1): 33–54. https://www.jstor.org/stable/ 25798813.

UNICEF. 2025. *Earthquake Flash Update No. 15*. 13 June. Accessed 29 November 2025. https:// www.unicef.org/myanmar/reports/unicef-myanmar-earthquake-flash-update-no-15.

United Nations Development Programme (UNDP). 2023. *Seeking Opportunities Elsewhere: Exploring the lives and challenges of Myanmar migrant workers in Thailand*. Accessed 29 November 2025. https://myanmar.un.org/en/254675-seeking-opportunities-elsewhere-exp loring-lives-and-challenges-myanmar-migrant-workers.

United Nations Development Programme (UNDP). 2024. *Poverty and the Household Economy of Myanmar: A disappearing middle class*. Accessed 29 November 2025. https://www.undp.org/ sites/g/files/zskgke326/files/2024-05/undp_poverty_and_the_household_economy_of_my anmar_-_a_disappearing_middle_class_april_2024_0.pdf.

United Nations High Commissioner for Refugees. 2024. ' Myanmar emergency update (as of end November 2024)', 20 December. Accessed 29 November 2025. https://reliefweb.int/report/ myanmar/myanmar-emergency-update-end-november-2024.

United States Institute of Peace. 2025. *The current situation in Burma* (Fact Sheet). Accessed 29 November 2025. https://reliefweb.int/report/myanmar/current-situation-burma-usip-fact-sheet.

University World News. 2021. 'Students join armed groups to fight military crackdown', 8 April. Accessed 29 November 2025. https://www.universityworldnews.com/post.php?story=202 1040820504572.

Vrieze, Paul. 2023. 'Joining the Spring Revolution or charting their own path? Ethnic minority strategies following the 2021 Myanmar coup', *Asian Survey* 63 (1): 90–120. https://doi. org/10.1525/as.2022.1717596.

Wa Lone, Poppy McPherson and Shoon Naing. 2025. 'Few doctors, throttled aid: How Myanmar's junta worsened earthquake toll', Reuters, 7 May. Accessed 27 November 2025. https://www. reuters.com/world/asia-pacific/few-doctors-throttled-aid-how-myanmars-junta-worsened-earthquake-toll-2025-05-07/.

Walton, Matthew J. 2016. *Buddhism, Politics and Political Thought in Myanmar*. Cambridge: Cambridge University Press. https://doi.org/10.1017/9781316659144.

Walton, Matthew J. and Aye Thein. 2023. 'Ethnic politics: Diversity and agency amidst persistent violence'. In *Myanmar: Politics, economy and society*, edited by Adam Simpson and Nicholas Farrelly, 31–45. London: Routledge.

Wells, Tamas. 2021. *Narrating Democracy in Myanmar: The struggle between activists, democratic leaders and aid workers*. Amsterdam: Amsterdam University Press.
Wilson, Trevor. 2016. *Eyewitness to Early Reform in Myanmar*. Asian Studies Series Monograph. Canberra: ANU Press. https://doi.org/10.26530/OAPEN_607553.
Wong, Mary Shepard and David Kareng. 2023. 'Creativity in crisis: Re-envisioning higher education in Myanmar's Spring Revolution', *The Asia-Pacific Education Researcher* 33: 1095–1103. https://doi.org/10.1007/s40299-023-00776-4.
World Bank. 2023. *Education in Myanmar: Where are we now?*. Accessed 29 November 2025. https://thedocs.worldbank.org/en/doc/716418bac40878ce262f57dfbd4eca05-0070012023/original/State-of-Education-in-Myanmar-July-2023.pdf/.
World Bank. 2024. *Educational Access and Disparities in Myanmar*. Accessed 29 November 2025. https://openknowledge.worldbank.org/entities/publication/fff8207c-1dec-45f2-9228-6388581bcee8.
World Bank. 2025. *Global Rapid Post-Disaster Damage Estimation (GRADE) Report Myanmar Earthquake – March 28, 2025*. Accessed 29 November 2025. https://www.preventionweb.net/publication/global-rapid-post-disaster-damage-estimation-grade-report-myanmar-earthquake-march-28.
Ye Myo Hein. 2022. 'Understanding the People's Defense Forces in Myanmar', United States Institute of Peace, 3 November. Accessed 27 November 2025. https://www.scribd.com/document/700418881/usip-org-Understanding-the-Peoples-Defense-Forces-in-Myanmar.
Ye Myo Hein. 2023. 'Myanmar's military is smaller than commonly thought – and shrinking fast', United States Institute of Peace, 4 May. Accessed 27 November 2025. https://www.usip.org/publications/2023/05/myanmars-military-smaller-commonly-thought-and-shrinking-fast.
Ye Myo Hein. 2024. 'Myanmar's resistance is making major advances', United States Institute of Peace, 14 August. Accessed 27 November 2025. https://www.scribd.com/document/700418780/usip-org-Myanmars-Military-Is-Smaller-Than-Commonly-Thought-and-Shrinking-Fast.
Younger, Holly. 2025. 'Myanmar turns down Taiwan quake rescue offer', *Taipei Times*, 31 March. Accessed 29 November 2025. https://www.taipeitimes.com/News/taiwan/archives/2025/03/31/2003834378.
Zöllner, Hans-Bernd. 2009. *Neither Saffron nor Revolution: A commentated and documented chronology of the monks' demonstrations in Myanmar in 2007 and their background, Part I*. Südostasien Working Papers 36. Berlin: Department of Southeast Asian Studies, Humboldt University. Accessed 22 March 2025. https://www.burmalibrary.org/en/neither-saffron-nor-revolution-part-1.
Zue Wadi Htun. 2020. 'Motivated but overstretched: Job satisfaction among Myanmar's university teachers', *Tea Circle: A Forum for New Perspectives on Burma/Myanmar*. Accessed 22 March 2025. https://teacircleoxford.com/2020/12/17/motivated-but-overstretched-job-satisfaction-among-myanmars-university-teachers/.

Index

Italic page numbers denote figures, **bold** page numbers denote tables and references to notes are given using n.